BEST CONTEMPORARY MONOLOGUES FOR KIDS AGES 7–15

THE APPLAUSE ACTING SERIES

BEST CONTEMPORARY MONOLOGUES FOR KIDS AGES 7–15

EDITED BY LAWRENCE HARBISON

APPLAUSE
THEATRE & CINEMA BOOKS
An Imprint of Hal Leonard Corporation

Published in 2015 by Applause Theatre & Cinema Books
An Imprint of Hal Leonard Corporation
7777 West Bluemound Road
Milwaukee, WI 53213

Trade Book Division Editorial Offices
33 Plymouth St., Montclair, NJ 07042

Permissions can be found on page 145, which constitutes an extension of this copyright page.

Printed in the United States of America

Book design by John J. Flannery

Library of Congress Cataloging-in-Publication Data

Best contemporary monologues for kids ages 7-15 / edited by Lawrence Harbison.
    pages cm
 Includes bibliographical references and index.
 ISBN 978-1-4950-1177-1 (pbk. : alk. paper)
1. Monologues--Juvenile literature. 2. Acting--Auditions--Juvenile literature. 3. Children's writings, American. 4. Children--Drama. 5. Teenagers--Drama. I. Harbison, Lawrence, editor.
 PN2080.B4125 2015
 808.82'45--dc23
                            2015022935

www.applausebooks.com

CONTENTS

M = male role
F = female role

INTRODUCTION

This anthology contains seventy-five challenging monologues for kids. All have subject matter appropriate for production in schools, much of it "serious and challenging," which will, I believe, interest child performers without offending administrators, teachers, or parents. Some are comic (laughs), some are dramatic (no laughs), some are seriocomic (some laughs).

There are wonderful monologues here by some of our finest playwrights, such as Don Nigro, Cassandra Lewis, Reina Hardy, Kayla Cagan, Jenny Lyn Bader, Eric Coble, Glenn Alterman, Constance Congdon and Barbara Dana, and by exciting up-and-comers such as Sharon Goldner, Gabriel David, Deanna Alisa Ableser, Martha Patterson, David Eliet, Connie Schindewolf, Mark Lambeck, and Phoebe Farmer. Most are from plays. Some are original pieces written for this book. The age of each character is given, but don't let that deter you if you like the monologue, as many could be done by a kid not that age.

Break a leg!

Lawrence Harbison
Brooklyn, NY

ALISON
Martha Patterson

Comic
ALISON, 13

ALISON *is talking to herself and her teddy bear in the mirror in her bedroom while putting on mascara. She also has a jar of cold cream and a box of tissues.*

ALISON   Today is my thirteenth birthday! Alison Jameson Michaels, happy birthday to me! And in honor of my thirteenth birthday . . . I am going to put on mascara!

[*To the teddy bear, stroking him:*]

Well, Bear, I don't know if you care about mascara. That's okay. I still love you. My mother doesn't think I should put goop on my face, and that's what she calls it—"goop." Helloooo? Everyone wears a little makeup. Well, not Emily. But she's a tool. Her mother probably wouldn't let her wear a miniskirt, even.

[*To teddy bear:*]

My mother also doesn't like me wearing jewelry to school. It's only plastic bracelets. She says it's "inappropriate" for young girls.

[*Putting on more mascara.*]

Know what, Bear? Once I found my mother reading my diary. She ripped out a page where I said something bad about her. Guess it hurt her feelings. But how was I to know she'd read it? It was supposed to be private. She has a terrible temper and she sends me to my room all the time, saying things like, "You're being *shrill.*" Well. I'll probably be just like my mother when I'm all grown up. Gardening in my backyard and wanting my daughter to "behave." But not now. I want to be a free spirit, like Beyoncé. All my friends feel the same way. Except Emily, my science partner. She thinks I'm a snob. I'm not a snob, not hardly. But she hasn't figured that out yet. Too much of a tool, like I said. My guidance counselor says I need to spend more time on my studies. Huh. What does she know? If only I cared more about biology and math. But I really don't care at all. When I had to dissect a frog it, like, totally grossed me out. Emily was really into the frog. I mean, *really* into it—this dead animal. Yuk.

[*Looks in the mirror.*]

Shoot. Maybe I should wash this stuff off. It's making me look goofy. What do you think, Bear? I don't want guys thinking I'm coming on to them or anything. I don't want to look like I'm *trying*.

[*Readjusts the mirror on the stand. Takes some cold cream from the jar and wipes her face with a tissue.*]

I think I still like being a kid. I like *you*, Bear. And maybe someday I'll give you up altogether, but not right now. Not on my thirteenth birthday when I'm not even halfway through being a teenager. I guess Mom's right. I should respect what she says. Isn't that one of the Ten Commandments? "Honor thy father and mother?"

[*Hugs Bear.*]

Today I am going to be a "Girl without Makeup." I like being natural. It's like yesterday, when I was only twelve. When I was still a kid. When I had my whole life ahead of me. I'll do it just to honor Mom. And to honor me.

ALMOST 16
Gabriel Davis

Dramatic
ANDREA, 15

*ANDREA's dad is sick. He wasn't supposed to be home . . . and she
had planned to "borrow" the car.*

ANDREA   Dad, let me take the car myself. I know that technically my learner's permit requires you in the car with me.
Technically, I have to wait two weeks to get my license, but
you know I can drive, you told me I'm better than Mom. I
can three-point turn, parallel park, and I observe the traffic
laws like a religion. So it's not like irresponsible to let me
drive, because you know I'm awesome at it. The coolest
girls in school, the one's whose parents are all probably
making huge donations at Mom's gala tonight, who live in
the massive houses on the hill and won't talk to me! They
started talking to me. Because they needed a ride to the
dance. And I'm like, I can take you. And they're like, "You're
sixteen?" and I'm all "Yeah." And then they said, "Cool." And
I've been eating lunch with them every day this week,
and they're all so excited. You and Mom were supposed to
be at her benefit gala thing tonight . . . you weren't supposed to have a stupid fever and be stuck at home. If I let
them down . . . If I don't get in that car right now and go
pick them up and take them to the dance . . . I'm dead, or I
might as well be. They will make it their life's work to ruin
me. I will be marked, mocked, and probably shunned. My
entire high school experience will become hell. I'm not
being dramatic. I'm being accurate, Dad. This is how things
go. So I'm begging you . . . just . . . . just go to sleep. You
have a fever, you know. You need your rest. Just, go to sleep

now and I'll . . . I'll still be here when you wake up in exactly three hours. Right before Mom gets back. Please, Dad. My life depends on it.

AMALIA'S WOODLAND ADVENTURE
Cassandra Lewis

Dramatic
ODIN THE OWL, can be any age, male or female

A young girl named AMALIA *is searching for her lost dog in the woods and meets a talking owl.*

ODIN THE OWL   One night when I was just a baby owl, an owlet, I was perched in my nest way up in a tree. My mother flew out into the night to find some supper for me, as she did every night. But as I was counting the stars and waiting for her to return, I had the feeling that I was not alone, that someone was watching me. Suddenly, I discovered just two branches down from me, the biggest bobcat I have ever seen. He glared at me and growled. At this point I had never flown by myself. But I knew I had to get away fast, so I concentrated really hard and up and away I flew. I was so amazed that I was actually able to fly that I didn't pay attention to where I was going. Pretty soon I was lost in the dark forest. I remembered what my mother taught me. She said if ever you are lost, find a safe place to stop and call for help. So I swooped down and landed on a tree branch, way up high where I could see all around me. I hooted until I got a response. A few minutes later, my Uncle Phil flew to my rescue. What I learned that night was to always pay attention to my surroundings and that I'm never truly alone. Sometimes you have to ask for help from others and that's okay. Just as others will help you—you will return the favor by helping others. Now night is falling and it's time for you to find your way back home. I will enlist some friends to help you.

ANNIE JUMP AND THE LIBRARY OF HEAVEN
Reina Hardy

Comic
ANNIE, 13

ANNIE JUMP, a 13-year-old science genius living in a small town, has just found out about a cruel, humiliating prank that some local boys have played on her mentally unstable, alien-obsessed father. In this monolog, ANNIE, who tries to be resigned to her father's weirdnesses, introduces herself to the audience, and is interrupted when a mysterious object falls from the sky.

ANNIE   I'm Annie Jump, and this whole story is about me. I'm thirteen years old, I'm about to go to high school in the fall, and I've lived in Strawberry, Kansas, for most of my life. My mom is from Chicago but she's dead now. She died when I was three and I don't miss her at all. I'm not mean, I just don't remember. It's not easy being a teenage science genius in a small town, especially when your dad believes in aliens. I try to take comfort in the thought that, even if he was totally and completely normal, no one would like me anyway. I mean, I have a 185 IQ. I took the SATs when I was ten, and I got a perfect score. Last year, I put a hard-boiled egg into orbit. Do you think there's anything in the world I could do to prevent Peter Stockholm and his cronies from stealing my gym shorts, short of being totally and completely someone other than me? Didn't think so. Anyway, it might be packed with mouth-breathers and oil brats, it might have a totally laughable high school chemistry lab and no Starbucks, it might only have one yoga class a week—church basement, 5:00 p.m., Fridays—but if there's one advantage to living in the middle of absolute nowhere, it's that Strawberry, Kansas, has a dark-sky rating of 2. And on the first night of the Perseids, when the moon is new, there's no city on Earth that can compare. If you sneak out of your room and go out to Hamlin's field at midnight and look up, you don't see planes, or pollution, or a bunch of buildings glowing on the horizon. You only see the stars, and the meteors, and . . .

[*She hears something.*]

What is that? What butt-wipe is setting off fireworks during a meteor shower?

BASKETBALL THERAPY
Gabriel Davis

Seriocomic
RYAN, 15

RYAN is in the office of a therapist. He tells the therapist that he doesn't need him to help him deal with losing his father, because he has basketball.

RYAN I don't need therapy! I don't need to be here. I'm not insane, I'm Linsane. As in, I've got a condition called "Lin-sanity!" And anyone in their right mind who has seen point guard Jeremy Lin do his thing on the basketball court would have it, too! That's what my mom and sister don't get. That's why they wanted me to come talk to you. But I don't need to be here. I'm only here because my mom caught me talking about Jeremy Lin at my father's wake. I never would have said anything, but out of the blue my cousin Arnie is like, "Jeremy Lin's a passing fad." If my dad had heard that, he'd have jumped out of that coffin and whopped Arnie. I actually looked over at Dad, lying there in our living room, wearin' his Sunday best, I half expected to see him get up. Of course he didn't, so I had to tell Arnie myself how Lin's got this low dribble that throws the defense, how his pick and rolls and combinations driving to the net are sick. Arnie tells me the only reason he's getting any attention is because he's like one of the first few Asians in basketball. Oh boy, I thought. Dad would have kicked Arnie out of the house by now. But I didn't, I just got into I guess a slightly, ah, heated debate with him where I like dared him to a game of air basketball in the mudroom. That's around the time some of the relatives said it seemed insensitive of me to go and play air basketball in the mudroom with everyone else trying to mourn and pay their respects and honestly I don't even care. It was my dad. I'm the most relative to the situation, if you know what I mean. So then, for the next two weeks Lin just continued to kick major ass and I couldn't pull myself away to do all these family activities. Lin was on fire and you know, my dad would have been pumped. Mom had this dinner in honor of him and I . . . I said I felt sick so I could stay home and watch the game. Dad would never have gone to some dinner with this game going on. Before Lin even made it to the NBA, my dad saw him back in the day. Dad followed college ball too, and knew how good Lin was at Harvard. When Lin first made it to the NBA and was struggling a bit, Dad would talk about how Lin just hadn't found his stride yet but he had greatness inside. Dad and I could talk about basketball for hours. So I guess that's why I . . . I just don't want to stop talking about basketball you know? To be honest, as long as I'm shootin' air hoops in the mud room and cuttin' up with Arnie, and watching the games like a religion . . . it doesn't even feel like he's gone. That's what they all can't understand. I'm not insensitive . . . I'm . . . They all want to be sad he's gone, see? But he's not. I'm with him, I'm keeping him with me. So . . . if they sent me here so I'd stop, well . . . I'm not going to stop talking about or watching basketball. They think I need this . . . talk therapy, but I already got it, you know. So, um . . . you follow basketball at all?

BEAT UP SUMMER
Barry Ernst

Dramatic
ANDY, 12

After running into a spooky, old, abandoned hotel with two other boys (and escaping from some older kids who are out to get them), ANDY makes up a grandiose story about three boys exactly their age being murdered by older kids. He scares them and himself, too!

ANDY   Don't you follow the news? They found three little boys with their throats cut last week somewhere in California. A small town like ours. In the woods by a river. They think it was a grown-up. A killer. A man who liked to kill kids. But it might have been other kids. They always blame everything on adults. We have to be careful. Those three kids who got murdered weren't. This is what probably happened. They had their bikes and just went down the wrong street. And those older kids were waiting for them. And when the older kids saw them, they blocked them off so they couldn't get by. And then took out their knives and went towards them. Slowly they crept, step by step. And when the little kids tried to run away, there was no place to go. And they caught them and then took them into the woods. And said to them, "You call us names and like to make fun of us. And throw things like crap at us! And use bad language and think it's funny. And call our mothers bad names. Did you really think we'd never catch you?" Then the biggest kid smiled and went over to the smallest boy and put his knife to his throat. The other kids thought he was just trying to scare them. But he was really mad. And then he cut his throat! And then the other kids probably said something like this: "You killed him! What do we do with him, now!" So he smiled and went over to the other little kids and killed them, too. Sliced their throats just like that!

[*Does a slicing motion with his hands.*]

It took only a second to kill them. And then he said to the other big kids, "And if you ever tell anyone about this, I'll come and get you, too!" And so all of them got on their bikes and got out of there as fast as they could go. I made it up, but that's probably what could have happened.

BEFORE THE LIGHT CHANGES
Robin Rice Lichtig

Dramatic
ALICE, 14

It is early morning in the kitchen of Clear Comfort, ALICE's family home on Staten Island, New York, in 1885. ALICE is speaking to the family cook.

ALICE   I don't want breakfast, Mildred. The sun's getting high. I need to get my camera set up before the light changes. Before the dew evaporates. Before Grandpa finishes reading *The Times* out on the porch. Before it's too late. [*Pause.*] I don't want scrambled eggs! You don't understand. Nobody understands. Yesterday I was right in the middle of washing a negative plate under the pump when Grandpa taps me on the shoulder. He wants to take a walk. I'm trying to concentrate. "Don't you care about anything but taking photographs?" he says. Jeez! With his bad leg, he should rest. With his bad heart, he shouldn't walk so much anyway. Julia and Violet think I should rather go shopping than take photographs. Mama thinks I don't give a hoot about anybody but myself. I do too! I give a hoot about lots of things. I care about little kids who live in other parts of New York and don't have a yacht club next door. And mothers who have to work. And Little Rufus and Big Rufus who pick Japanese beetles off the peonies and mow our grass and and and trim the sea grass back from . . . I care! And you, Mildred, you make the best sour candies in the whole world despite unfortunate bouts with flatulence. I care about you and all our servants. And and and sick people. And old people like Mr. Van deVere who got stuck in the marsh. I care about our garden, the sky, the river, ships that pass, gulls, egrets, dragonflies, changing seasons. I care about every second, every inch, every breath of it all. I care so much, I want it to last forever. Sometimes I sit on the Linden tree bench and look at the river and think about this. About how seconds come and go and flow out into the ocean . . . and they're gone forever. I'm going to take a picture of the dew on the wisteria on the pergola at this very moment in time. Grandpa in his rocker under the wisteria, reading the *Times*. I'm going to take that picture before the light changes and it's gone.

BENJAMIN

Deanna Alisa Ableser

Dramatic
BENJAMIN, 12 to 14

BENJAMIN *is average looking. He dresses nicely, his hair is nicely done, and he takes good care of his appearance. He is speaking to a psychiatrist who his parents forced him to go see, thinking that he is simply being a "moody' teenager."*

BENJAMIN   You think boys aren't affected by it, you know. You think that we're strong and manly and nothing really gets to us. If only you really knew . . . I mean, really knew. Sure, the girls cry and then head off to the school counselor and bawl their eyes out there, but we're just as messed up as they are. You know, we're human too. I remember when they first told me about it. They took me out to dinner and we were going to have a "special family meal." Yeah, right. It was special . . . super special. "Benny dear, you know your father and I will always love you no matter what, right?" What type of talk is this during our special family meal? Great, yeah, you both love me, no matter what . . . now where is my ultimate burger with extra sauce? Loaded chili french fries? Megasized soda? "Benny honey, let's be serious here. You're a big boy . . . I mean, a teenager, almost an adult." [*Beat.*] I shut my mouth. I knew I wasn't going to like what was going to come out of my mom's mouth . . . and my dad, well, he was just sitting there . . . well, just looking sad. Look, I didn't break anything or ruin anything that can't be replaced, my grades will go up by next semester, I swear I didn't . . . "Benny sweetheart, it's not about you. You're just great. Your daddy and I will always love you, no matter what." [*Beat.*] Okay, so I couldn't help it then . . . the tears started slowly. I'm not proud of losing it . . . I'll admit that. But, you see, once I started, I really couldn't stop. [*Beat.*] "Look, Mom, I won't fight and argue anymore. You and Dad won't have to worry about me! I'll sit and be quiet and be a great kid from this moment forward. Please, whatever you need, I'll do. I'll get an extra job so there's no money problems. I'll make you breakfast in bed every day until I'm off to college. I'll clean up the dog's stuff until . . . " "Benny, it's not about you . . . your father and I just can't live to-gether anymore . . . we'll always love you. Remember that, no matter what, we will always love you." [*Beat.*] "Look, guys . . . you're adults . . . you can work it out . . . you've always fought all the time . . . just keep on fighting for another forty years and it'll work out . . . come on, you can do it. I know you can.

THE BOY WHO CRIED WEREWOLF
Daniel Guyton

Comic
CHRIS, 8 to 9

CHRIS is a third-grade boy, telling his classmates about the were-wolf he saw last night.

CHRIS   I saw one last night. I was in my room doing my homework, and I heard a dog howling—or at least I thought it was a dog. But when I looked out my window, I saw the dog standing on his hind legs! And he was wearing a bowling shirt. And pants. And he had a hat on that said "Nike." Or maybe it was "Mike"? I couldn't really see it. But anyways, he looked like a man kinda, but . . . but really hairy. Kinda like your dad, Benny. But younger and skinnier, I think. Anyway, his clothes were ripped, and his eyes were really yellow. And he had teeth. Like really long teeth. Like . . . like the way a dog's teeth look, you know, and . . . and then he saw me. He looked right at me, and my whole body went numb. And I wanted to run, but I couldn't move. I just stood there, staring at him. And then he howled. It was the loudest sound I had ever heard in my life, and my entire room shook. It even broke the glass on my iPad. So I ran as fast as I could down the hall into my mom's room, but . . . my mom wasn't there. And then I heard the window break in my bedroom. So I immediately crawled under my mom's bed! I expected something to grab my leg, or bite me, or to rip me to pieces. But . . . then everything went quiet. The noises all stopped for . . . what seemed like forever. And then suddenly I heard screaming. It was my neighbor, Mrs. London. She kept on yelling that someone ate her cat. Just over and over—"Someone ate my cat! Someone ate my

cat." It was horrible. I thought she was joking at first, but
. . . finally I looked out my mom's window, and I saw Mrs.
London yelling. But the dog . . . or man . . . wasn't there. But
it wasn't a dog or a man at all, you guys. It was . . . it was a
werewolf.

BUT FOR THE GRACE . . .
FACES OF HUNGER IN AMERICA
David Eliet

Dramatic
BOBBY, 7 to 9

BOBBY *is sitting on a box or on the floor in a food pantry, talking to a social worker. He has a small bag out of which he pulls a battery-powered toothbrush still in its plastic packaging. He pulls out a cheap little red plastic car. Finally, he pulls out a package of Oreos.*

BOBBY   [*Holding out the Oreos.*] I told the pantry man I don't have no money to pay. He said I didn't have to. Said he was givin' 'em to me. Mom was gettin' her bags of food an' stuff, an' he just handed 'em to me. "Here you go, son," he said. Said they was a present.

[*Carefully sets down the Oreos and picks up the toothbrush.*]

See this. Got a battery. Goin' to brush my teeth real good now. Just like my friend Jason. He's got one just like this. It goes . . .

[*Makes sound of the toothbrush.*]

Zzzzzzzzz. Zzzzzzzzz. Zzzzzzzzz. An' your teeth feel all kinda tingly.

[*He sets down the toothbrush and picks up the car.*]

I sure do need this.

[*Looking at the car.*]

I had me a whole lot of cars from the Salvation Army Santa. An' there was one kinda like this. Only it kinda got smushed when I stepped on it. Mama said it was my own fault, 'cause of never pickin' up after myself. I've been wantin' a car just like this one real bad now almost forever, 'cause red's my favoritist color.

[*Sets the car down and picks up the Oreos.*]

I'm not gonna open them now. I'm gonna save 'em for school. That's what I'm gonna do. 'Cause you know what? When we have snack time, an all the other kids are pullin' out the real good stuff, like them packages of cheese an' crackers, an' I got nothin' 'cept for somethin' my Mama made up herself. An' everyone's always kinda pointin' an' sayin', "What's that? Ain't you got nothin' good?" An' sometimes it makes me feel kinda bad.

[*Leaning forward, confidentially.*]

Kinda like havin' to come to the food pantry, 'cause it's kinda 'barrassin'. I mean I don't never want Jason to know, 'cause then he might stop bein' my friend. Mama says if that happened, then it would show he wasn't no real friend in the first place. But I don't know, 'cause he never says nothin' mean about my clothes, like some a the other kids on the first day of school, when they're all wearin' their new jeans, an' sneakers, an' backpacks, an' stuff, an I'm wearin' somethin' from the used clothes places. Some a them can be real kinda mean 'bout it, too. But Jason don't hardly say a word, an' he's still my best friend.

[*Picks up the Oreos, starts to open them. Stops.*]

No. I gotta save 'em. I gotta show 'em. I gotta show them other kids I got me some good food for snack time.

CANNONBALL
Kayla Cagan

Dramatic
ALEX, 12

ALEX *is talking to the neighborhood pool lifeguard about his/her behavior at the pool that day.*

ALEX   I wasn't trying to hurt myself. I love swimming. I've been on Swim Team forever, at least since first grade. You know that. I didn't jump in the shallow end like that to scare the other kids. You know Brian's mom, Mrs. Greenbaum? Well, she called me over. I didn't want to get out of the pool, because I was messing around with Manuel and Emma and a bunch of the other kids and we were just having fun—but I got out anyway. I grabbed my towel and wrapped it around me because I was soaking wet. I shook my hair, wiping the water out of my eyes and ears, and I walked over. I said hi. I figured she was going to ask me something about Brian or school or whatever but instead she did this weird thing. She called over Mrs. Taylor and Ms. McKenzie. They were sipping their iced teas and sat down on the bench by her. They looked like they did when they cheered for us at swim meets, all excited. So, Mrs. Greenbaum said, "Hi, Alex. How are you doing?" And I answered, "Fine. Thanks." And she said, "No, really . . . How are you doing?" And I answered her again, "Fine. I'm good. I'm cold!" I shook a little and all the moms laughed. And then she said, "Alex, how are you really doing? Like with your parents' divorce? It must be so rough on you." And then I just kind of stood there. I couldn't believe she really just asked me that. That was weird, right? And mean? The other moms were looking at me over their drinks. Their eyes were so big they could have popped out of their heads. "I'm fine," I answered. "I'm fine." "Isn't that amazing?" Mrs. Greenbaum said to Mrs. Taylor and Ms. McKenzie, like I did some amazing thing. "Can I get back in the water now?" I asked. "I'm really cold." "Of course," Mrs. Greenbaum said. And that's when I dropped my towel on the bench and ran back to the pool and cannonballed into the shallow end as hard as I could. I didn't want to hurt the other kids. I didn't want to hurt myself. I just wanted to disappear.

CATS?

Shirley King

Comic
CASSIDY, 14

CASSIDY is a brilliant science student on a mission. Her scheme to thwart the evil Frost Gang hits a snag, until she suddenly gets a brainstorm. What if she just adds cats?

CASSIDY   All along the Eastern Seaboard we can expect an early frost. You heard it here first. The Frost Mob is on the move. They've mutated, and furthermore they're like, digitized! Totally! I am not making this up. Using a high-frequency binary code, they can mess big-time with the Universe. Trust me, now's the time for action. One problem: I need to have a plan. How can I trash those terminators? Wish I knew. Oh. Maybe I do. How about adding cats? You know, little furry purr machines? Why? Because in a binary code, each digit is represented by a string and—pay attention now, this is important—this string is viewed as a fatal number in Secret Code circles. NOW—what do we know about cats? They love chewing cords and strings. I am not making this up. My cat Oliver actually ate the cord to my computer mouse. So if I sent cats to chomp those binary code strings—what else do we know about cats? Independent? Right. So I can't just order them to shred those binary strings. BUT cats hear sounds way higher in frequency than we do. So what'd I tell you about binary codes? Can you say high frequency? Good! AND we all know that cats can hear paint peeling ten miles away. Here's my plan: I'll act like a turncoat. You know, someone who passes on secret information for a price. And THEN I'll offer to give the Frost Gang secret information IF they meet me at the cattery.

Then—yes! I'll turn those cats loose! Low tech? Uh huh, but this plan just might work. Why? Because while dying to get secret information, the Frost Mob actually might forget to guard their binary string from cats. Know what that means? I get to save the universe! SO—here I go! Frost Mob, beware! For I will be packing fur!

THE CHILDREN'S CRUSADE
Jenny Lyn Bader

Seriocomic
CHRIS, 12

CHRIS *is a child, male or female, who is feeling bitter about a parental punishment. This monologue is addressed to the parent who has meted out the punishment.*

CHRIS   James VI was crowned King of Scotland when he was one year old. Louis XIV was five when he became King of France. So I . . . should be able to take the bus by myself. Okay, maybe I used a strong word, but . . . According to history? All your rules make no sense. The videos you won't let me watch because they're too violent? Kids were at once a major part of official violence! An army of kids marched across Europe in the thirteenth century. The Children's Crusade. Sure, it didn't turn out too well for most of them, but . . . it was a whole war. For kids! Joan of Arc—visited by visions when she was twelve, then became a soldier. I'm as old as she was, and you don't even let me watch wars when they're on TV! I'm not saying I want to start a war. I'm saying I have all these words I'm not allowed to say, books I'm not allowed to read, movies I'm not allowed to see, while at another time I might have been in charge of—Macedonia! Look at K'ang-Hsi, emperor of China at seven . . . Tutankhamen, "King Tut," pharaoh of Egypt at nine. Right now I'm older than either of them, and you still won't let me take the bus. I know you think I'd miss my stop, but all I need is a chance to prove [*Interrupts self.*]—and yeah, I know you gave me one when you said you'd-let-me-take-the-bus-by-myself-next-time-if-I-just-got-off-at-the-right-stop, and I realize I messed that up. But my book got so good around

Seventy-Ninth Street . . . it was about the Roman Empire, which Constantine VII ruled the eastern part of when he was just five? Sure it looked bad when I missed our stop, and the . . . three . . . stops after that. But it wasn't a fair test. Because you were there. And you need to trust that if I were alone, I'd stop reading and be able to handle the—f . . . local bus! But you think I'm . . . This . . . idea that I'm a "child"—it's such a recently invented, technical category— can't you see that? How you always say I should play with the Altmans' kid, Danny . . . How I'd like him so much, since we're both twelve. Danny Altman collects worms! You think I'd like playing with someone I don't know, with completely different interests, simply because we're both twelve? Do I tell you to play with my gym teacher, Mr. Phelps, because you're both thirty-seven? No. I'd choose friends for you more thoughtfully. For a long time, this "child" thing didn't matter. No one cared. And I wouldn't be in a corner for say-ing one bad word at dinner. One F . . . f . . . frickin' bad word in a whole otherwise good discussion. You couldn't have put me here, because I would own this corner and all the rooms around it, as part of my kingdom. Because at one time, children would be given kingdoms, over which . . . We . . . would rule.

CLOCKS
Abbey Fenbert

Dramatic
ADA, 13

After discovering that ADA *has been studying the theories of evolution and relativity with John Galilee, her father, who is a preacher, is determined to save her soul. He wants her to have a profound encounter with God, and so he leaves her alone in the woods in the middle of the night. This is Ada's prayer.*

ADA   Daddy? Daddy! Don't you—don't you leave me here—don't you—

[*She falls to her knees, sobbing. Eventually, she stands and directs her appeals to God.*]

You out there? Huh? Well are ya? You got somethin' to say to me? You got wonder and knowledge? Well, tell it then! What are you waitin' for? Tell me everything—tell me the truth—shoot it down! Tell me what moves faster than light. Tell me if there's a reason why nature selects what it does, what gets to live and what gets to die, and what we can become . . . And while you're at it, why don't you tell me what time's made of? And why'd you make a universe that don't sit still, this big unfurling ocean, all torn and warped, where's it end? Speak! How come everybody believes plain and easy that Jesus Christ turned water into wine, but no one wants to talk about matter turning into energy—about primates into homo sapiens—about light—about light . . . Why won't you answer? Why am I here alone? "Any ray of light moves with the determined velocity c whether the ray be emitted by a stationary or a moving body" . . . Swear by him that liveth . . . all things therein . . . swear by him . . . He that speaketh truth . . . Am I a piece of you? Of you? In the divine image created you me? Did you create everybody else but me? Am I something else altogether? Swear by him . . . Am I the variation life will not select? I wished for . . . I wished for knowledge and wonder.

COVENTRY CAROL

James McLindon

Seriocomic
IMOGENE, 7

IMOGENE *doesn't have school today. Yesterday, there was a school shooting. She talks to the audience.*

IMOGENE   This is the time we do art. I'm in first grade, although some people think I'm in second grade cuz I'm pretty mature. I looooove art. I would be a famous artist if I wasn't going to be a famous princess. Or a ballerina. My mom says I can't be a princess cuz she isn't a queen, but that I could still be a ballerina and then go to art school and be a famous artist after, and that's much better cuz princesses don't really do anything, except look pretty. Then my dad said, "Cheer up, Imogene Jelly-Bean"—my name is Imogene, he just says Jelly-Bean—"maybe you'll grow up and marry a prince and become a princess that way." That's when my mom stared at him. Like this.

[*She stares, sort of warning stare, with one eyebrow raised.*]

My dad said, "What?" but my mom wouldn't say what, so I don't know what. I wish we had school today so we could have art. I don't get boys. Sometimes they can be really nice, but sometimes Ms. Kerrigan says it's like someone just disconnected their brains from their bodies and their bodies have just realized that nobody's in charge and they should be silly before somebody hooks them back up to their brains. That's when she tells them they have to be aware of their bodies so no one gets hurt. So that's what I thought they were doing yesterday when they fell down. I don't get boys.

DELLA AND JOEY
Ellen Davis Sullivan

Dramatic
JOEY, 15

JOEY is speaking to his 17-year-old sister, Della, in her bedroom in their apartment in New York City. She's their mother's biological child. JOEY's adopted. The time is the fall of 2008.

JOEY   It's what Mom didn't do. She promised me she'd keep her damn job. No matter what happens, Joe, she says. Don't you worry. Even when all this Wall Street stuff starts and her company's all over the news. Yeah, you think I don't know what happens downtown? Just 'cause you only use your phone to post selfies and text your girls doesn't mean I'm not watching how it's going down there where our momma works. I gotta know. And she says, don't worry, Joe. Don't worry. Just keep studying. But I can't do that with what I'm seeing every day. The Dow's shedding points like dead umbrellas dumped in gutters. Whole banks gone. Did you know a whole bank can disappear? Not like 9/11, not windows shattering, glass flying—just like, bad numbers and more bad numbers, then people go to take their money out and, poof, the whole thing's vanished. Even when that's in the news day after day, she comes home every night and says, "Don't you worry, Joe. I'm safe. I won't lose my job." And you're not listening. You're just sitting there thumbs working like mad, eyes on your screen. Know why? 'Cause even if she loses her job, nothing's gonna change for you. But me, I'm just one worn-out sneaker away from being somebody completely different. You're her own kid. Nothing can happen to you. She can't afford tuition for private school? You'll do all right at Beacon High. Get

your As, find some new girls to hang with. Not me. I lose
Dalton, I'm dead. My only chance for college is graduating
from a place no one expects a kid like me to get through.
My head needs that prep school halo hanging around it,
or I'm just another basketball wannabe, hoping to stick in
college long enough to make the pros. Don't tell me I'm
just like you. I ain't never been just like you no matter how
much our momma loves me. You don't have to believe me,
but I know how I get looked at in stores, on the subway,
old white ladies flinching as I pass 'em on the sidewalk. Old
men in the park tugging on their dog's leash, like what,
I'm gonna grab some geezer's fur ball and run off with it?
Don't tell me I'll be fine. I won't. I know what this means. I'm
doomed.

EPSOM SALTS
Frank Higgins

Seriocomic
SARAH, 10

SARAH *tells us how she is going to help her mom relax. She has a bag of Epsom salts and a footbath filled with water.*

SARAH I'm sorry I had to stop playing, but my mom'll be home any minute and I wanna surprise her. My mom's not really mean, but working at Macy's makes her mean. It helps her be less mean if she can soak her feet. She needs to soak her feet a lot at Christmas. She says Christmas rush starts day after Thanksgiving and then gets worse and worse. You should hear her: "I've never had so many people be so rude to me in my life as at Christmastime. Just today a woman comes up when I'm swamped with customers and says, 'Would my husband like this shirt?' 'I don't know, ma'am, but many men do.' 'I don't care about other men; would my husband like this shirt?' 'I couldn't say, but you can always return it.' 'You're supposed to help people; you're a terrible clerk.'" And the woman goes away and puts in a complaint about my mom. This is called Epsom Salts. It helps your feet relax. My mom soaks her feet till the water's lukewarm, then has me bring more hot water. Christmastime takes two tubs of hot water before she can fix supper.

[*She stirs in the Epsom salts.*]

This is what Christmas does to people like my mom, but you don't hear about it. And right after Christmas, she says it's worse. She says day after Christmas the store's jammed with people trying to return stuff. You'd think people would be happy somebody gave 'em a gift, but they want the money. And you'd like to think people wouldn't try to get money for something they been wearing for a while; you'd like to think there's something inside that keeps people from doing that, and that's part of what Christmas is about. But my mom says it happens all the time. Cuz see, people know that day after Christmas they don't gotta have a receipt. She says people try to return clothes the store hasn't even had for two years. So she hates Christmas. She says it reminds you people can be cheats, even people you'd never think that about. So Christmas makes her sad. I bought my mom her Christmas present today. It's a big box of Epsom salts. I'm pretty sure she won't return it.

EVERYDAY PEOPLE
Debbie Lamedman

Dramatic
CARLY, 15

CARLY, *a high school freshman, has been the victim of cyberbullying. Her tormentors think her name is "Cowley." Here, she is filming herself talking directly to the people who have been targeting her.*

CARLY Um . . . I think this is the only way to talk to anyone. If I tried to talk to any of you . . . in person, I mean . . . you'd say something horrible or push me or hurt me or laugh at me. So I'm posting this on YouTube and I'm sure you'll all see it and maybe this way you'll listen.

[*Beat.*]

I don't know why you think I did what you say I did. I never stole anyone's boyfriend. I never said mean things about anyone. I don't really know any of you . . . why would I talk trash about people I don't even know? I'm not a slut. I'm not a bitch. I'm not any of those things you've called me. I've tried like crazy to ignore it all. The messages. The fake profile page. I've tried to pretend like it wasn't really happening. But it's impossible to do that. And there's no one to talk to about it. I don't have any friends. You've all made sure of that. Who am I gonna tell? Who would believe me? My mom would just tell me to ignore it . . . take the high road. Well, I've tried to do that. I've tried to ignore it and it doesn't work. It just gets worse and worse every day. I hate it here. I never wanted to move in the first place, and now . . . [*Beat.*] I hate it here. I don't belong here. I don't belong anywhere. I thought it would stop; I thought you would all stop hassling *me, but you're not stopping. Don't you have* anything better to do? I just don't understand why this is happening to me. I'm a good person. I'm tired of feeling sick to my stomach every single miserable day of my life. It's nonstop. And I can't take it anymore. I won't take it anymore. You won. Are you happy now? You all won. [Beat.] And my name isn't Cowley. It's Carly. I'm Carly.

[Beat.]

And now I'm leaving. For good. Thanks.

[Moves to turn off the camera and has one last thought.]

Ha . . . what am I saying "thanks" for?

FAITH

James McLindon

Dramatic
SIMON, 12

SIMON *fervently hopes to be God's prophet. He has just seen a beautiful, sad woman, whom he is sure is God's messenger to him, floating above the stage. He is telling her about his father, who left when he was very young.*

SIMON   Well, I feel like I should love him. I talked to him once. Almost. He called when I was, like, four, and I wanted to be really nice and funny and all, so he'd come back, but when my mom held out the phone to me, I got, I don't know, really mad and really scared and I wouldn't take it. And he never came back. But he might have. I just sort of blew it. But now I kind of hate him and hope he never comes back because when he left me, he made me feel all powerless. And then I felt bad about feeling all that about my own dad, so I tried to compensate by acting out instead of thinking about him. At least, that's what the school therapist in third grade told me I was feeling, cuz I had no idea why I was getting into trouble all the time. But God's different—you *have* to love God without ever meeting him. Don't you?

FAUX PAS
Elin Hampton

Dramatic
A STUDENT BOY or GIRL, 7

A student speaks to a teacher who has just admonished him or her for not doing the "correct assignment." The teacher has asked the student what he or she has drawn instead of what the teacher had assigned to the class. He or she holds up a drawing. It is of a house with a window upstairs and a dog in front.

BOY/GIRL STUDENT   It's a picture of my dog, Kramer. He's a pedigree mutt and he's the best brother in the whole wide world. Yeah, I know. I did hear you, but I didn't do it because I don't have a mommy. Elena, my babysitter—she has children but they're big, they live in their own houses, I think—she picks me up because my daddies have to be at work. They love each other and their names are Dad and Pop. They bought me. I mean they adopted me when I was a little, little, little baby so that we could be a family. They said that I was the best present they ever got. I was in a state named Kansas and they got a phone call saying how I was born, and then they went to pick me up and take me to their house, which is where I live.

[*Points to house in the picture.*]

This is it. That's my room up there. It's yellow, with a bean-bag chair and posters of horses. It has a bed in it for Kramer, but he likes to sleep with me instead. Pop named him for his favorite TV show that he watches on reruns. You don't know any of this because my real teacher, Mrs. Ripkey, had to move when her husband got a job in a plant, and then you came and now you're our new teacher. Maybe someone should have told you this so that you wouldn't have to cry when I don't make a Mother's Day card. But if it's okay, on Father's Day, can I make two cards?

FEARING: TALE OF A DREADFUL TOWN
Nicholas Priore

Dramatic
SARA, 10

SARA explains to her teacher, Mr. McCobb, why she fell asleep in class again today.

SARA   Still couldn't sleep tonight . . . not for the usual reason, though. It wasn't the scary feelin' this time . . . it was Mom's constant screamin', she just won't stop . . . must not be able to sleep either. Never heard sounds like that before, not from a person . . . it goes from a high screech to a low growl and every level in between. The hallway outside my room seems longer at night and it always feels like someone's creepin' around right behind me . . . I don't ever look back, though, and I squint past the mirrors because my face looks scary in the dark. Mom's screamin' got louder when I got to the stairs . . . the stairs are even scarier, I don't ever go down there at night time. I had to go see if Mom was okay, though . . . I closed my eyes even though she would say that's dangerous, but it feels safer in there, and so I grabbed the railing and went real slow. Every step felt like it might not be there, like I might fall forward into nothing and never stop falling . . . but then the steps flattened out into the floor, and I was downstairs, so I opened my eyes. Dad was asleep on the couch with that sad humming rain-bow screen left on the TV real loud, he can sleep through anything . . . and Mom was louder than ever. Louder and louder the closer I got to her door . . . and then it just stopped, silent as soon as I touched the doorknob, like she could sense me . . . like she was listening. My mom was always the one to make me feel better when I got scared—

she came in my room and stayed with me till I was sleepin'. Never thought I would be afraid to see her. I closed my eyes and opened the door . . . then I opened my eyes. She was sittin' straight up in bed starin' right at me with eyes that didn't look like hers, like she saw so many bad things that her eyes turned bad. Her head cocked a bit to the side, like an animal sizin' me up . . . and then she showed her rotten teeth. I wanted to ask her how she was, but I couldn't say anything . . . I could barely even move . . . but when she hurled herself off the bed and at the door, I slammed it shut before she got there . . . . . . I heard the sound of her smashing into the door as I ran back upstairs and hid under my covers . . . closed my eyes and covered my ears while she banged on that door the resta the night.

FROM FUNNY
Philip Dawkins

Comic
SON, 12

A 12-year old boy gives his bar mitzvah speech.

SON   Thank you Rabi Berg, thank you Rabi Porter. Thank you everyone for being here. Especially those of you who traveled from far away places like Florida and Alberta, which is in Canada. I know now is when I'm supposed to read my Torah portion, but if nobody minds, I think I'll just do a quick set instead.

[*He takes out his notebook, a pencil, and his cheat sheet.*]

I read somewhere that in order for something to be funny, it had to be painful and it had to happen a long time ago. If that's the case, then my Torah portion would be hilarious. A Guy and his Kid are at the bar. A man walks into the bar. Kid says to his Dad, "Hey, that man looks like Uncle Jim." Dad says, "That's not a man. That is your Uncle Jim." A Guy and his Kid walk into a bar. The bartender says, "I'm gonna need to see some I.D." The Guy shows him his military I.D. and the Kid pulls out his junior high I.D. Bartender says, "I hear it's really rough out there. Thank you for your service." The Guy says, "You're welcome." Bartender says, "I wasn't talking to you." A Guy, his Kid, and a Baby Goat walk into a bar. Bartender says, "Hey, no kids 'r animals!" The Baby Goat says, "But some animals 'r kids."

[*Wait. Wait. Kid crosses that joke off his set list, mouthing "Not funny" to himself.*]

Guy walks into a bar. Bartender says, "Hey." Kid walks into a bar. Bartender says, "Hey." A horse walks into a bar. Bartender says, "Hey." Horse says, "No thanks, I just ate." After my mom died, I asked Rabbi Porter, "Why? Why did this happen to us?" Rabbi Porter looks at me and says, "Son, if I knew the answer to that . . ." "Yes?" I said. "If I knew the answer to that . . . You think I'd give it away for free?!" When I decided I wanted to become a comedian, my dad bought me this book called *How to Be Funny, or This Book Is a Waste of Money*. No, seriously, that's what it's called. Anyway, the book talked about The Rule of Three. It said funny things always come in threes. A Priest, a Rabbi, and a Doctor. A Dog, a Cat, and a Monkey. A Boy, his Dad, and his Mom. That's funny. That's good. When there's three. But when there's two. It's just . . . it's nothing, you know? It's just one thing and another thing. A priest and a rabbi. A dog and a cat. A boy and his dad. That's not funny. That's just how it is. Once there was a family of three and they laughed a lot. Then they were a family of two and they had to try harder. Cuz funny is hard. Funny's real hard.

GAME CONSOLE
David L. Epstein

Dramatic
GENEVIEVE, 14

GENEVIEVE *has been watching Mack play Xbox for too long. In this monologue, she gives him an ultimatum.*

GENEVIEVE   I'm so sorry that you won't make it to the boss level, I really am! I've watched you play this stupid computer game for hours on end, every day, all summer long, and I'm completely sick of it! I can't do it for another minute! Don't you know why I come over here? Doesn't the thought even cross your mind? It certainly isn't to watch you hit buttons and scream at the screen! [*Beat.*] I come over here because I like you, Mack. I always have. And I thought there was something between us. Ever since we were young we've been close. Water balloon fights. Touch football. All those summer nights catching lightning bugs and playing in the yard . . . But I see it now. You are still dumb and immature and haven't realized what matters. You are just a kid and you'll keep going this way until you become one of those guys whose brains have turned to mush because you haven't opened a book in ten years—or maybe you won't even remember how to read! And women won't give you a second thought because it will be too late—they'll see exactly what you are because, by that point, they'll all have been through exactly what I'm going through now! Don't you see how lucky you've got it? Don't you see that I'm standing right in front of you? That I've been sitting beside you on this couch waiting for you to do something and you barely look my way? I can't do this anymore. I've waited so long. Boys call me, Mack. They call and e-mail and text

. . . What do you want? Hmm? What is important? Gaining experience points in a game? What about real life, Mack? Does experience matter there?

THE GIRL WHO SWALLOWED A CACTUS
Eric Coble

Dramatic
PEZ, 8 to 15

In this play, PEZ *(who may be played by either a male or female actor) is addressing the audience directly.*

PEZ   Someone had left it here. Just left it here. Beside the dirt road that ran behind Sheila's house was a pile of junk. Not just any junk. This was the sidebars of a swing set, the top bars of a monkey bars, the boards from a teeter-totter, an old red car hood—this big—a slide, a full long slide three times as long as Sheila, but just lying there on its side in the weeds, old chains, giant metal springs, and perhaps—no, definitely—the best piece of junk in the entire universe . . . an incinerator. A silver metal box about yay high, shaped like a rocket, but the top came off, on a hinge, and you could climb inside. Exactly like a rocket. It had been built to burn trash, and Sheila's mother, of course, being the reasonable, loving adult she was, didn't want her only daughter climbing in and being burnt to a crisp.

Parents. The only fire inside was in Sheila's mind! The thing was big enough for her and me and Leon and Dennis and maybe even the twins—they're little, they're wiry, they can fit into nooks and crannies, like rubber bands stuffed into the cracks in a desk. You know.

But who had left this all here? Why would you collect some of the best treasures in the world and just leave it here? No one knew. Mom seemed calm, maybe it was someone from the school nearby getting rid of old playground equipment. Although that doesn't explain the car hood. Or really, the incinerator. But where our mothers saw a pile of useless metal . . . Sheila (of course it was Sheila, Sheila who talked Dennis into wearing a black garbage bag to be a bat and hang from a rope and a tree over a model city that was to be destroyed with firecrackers, all to re-create a scene from a great Japanese monster movie she'd seen online, Sheila of the too-many-adventures-to-tell-you-off-today, that Sheila), *she* saw in that pile of junk . . . the foundations of a city. And she had one. Whole. Summer. To build it. Leon was the clever one with his hands, Dennis was strong as three second-graders, and the twins were fast and cheerful, and together they built it. Like this.

[*Constructs as he or she speaks.*]

We rested the swing set against the pinion tree by the dirt road. Then we hoisted the car hood up to rest on the base and the tree branches—the floor of our house. This high off the ground. So of course we needed a ladder. Ladder, ladder, ladder . . . What to use as a ladder . . . the monkey bars! Right! We set them on end . . . Voila! Ladder! We got old cardboard boxes from Leon's uncle's basement to make walls around the floating car hood so it was a room, and ran the teeter-totter boards across the air from the car hood and branches to the incinerator top. And we lifted the slide . . . propped it against the tree . . . in case they needed a quick escape down from the fort. Wooop! Except even the twins could see the slide wouldn't support their weight were they to actually sit on it. It would function more as a fast elevator than slide. And result in more bruised bottoms than would be ideal. That was Monday. There was much to be done, but this . . . This was a fine start.

THE GIRL WHO SWALLOWED A CACTUS
Eric Coble

Dramatic
PEZ, 8 to 15

In this play, PEZ (who may be played by either a male or female actor) is addressing the audience directly.

PEZ   We were all sprawled in the dirt and weeds in the darkness. The twins—"hee hee hee" as per usual—waiting for the next car to drive down the dirt road. We'd get a warning from the headlights. This time Dennis swore the second he saw the headlights, he would be the first one up the ladder into the car-hood-swing-set-monkey-bar tree fort. Sheila knew he was wrong. She'd been eating nothing but Froot Loops all evening (did I mention how GRAND it was being without a mother for a weekend?). And she knew she had the energy to get to the fort first. The whole point was to get in, just barely get in before the passing car lights slid over you and you were caught. So you knew you were tucked safe in the fort and the passing car would have no idea you were there. Desert Ninjas. Or Giggling Desert Ninjas in the twins' case.

But so there we all were when Leon yells "CAR!" It wasn't even Dennis who saw it, how on earth did he expect to get the jump on everyone like that? But Leon: "CAR!" And we RUN!

Like mice exploding from a cheese house, like water drops exploding from a water balloon hitting the asphalt, BOOM.

All these little bodies run, run, run, run up the monkey

bar ladder—lights getting closer—the twins onto the car hood—lights closer—Leon up and behind the cardboard wall—the lights on the tree now—Sheila's in, she tries to give Dennis a hand . . .

[*As Sheila:*] "The lights are ON you, Dennis!"

But she pulls him up, twins "Hee hee hee," Leon "Shut up," Shut up!" and the car—or rather truck, it had to be a truck it was so loud and heavy—RUUMMMMMBLING by on the dirt and rock road and we all clump silent, a clump of breath and dirty clothes "hee hee hee" "shut up!" The truck is going past us in the dark as all the other cars ever did, "hee hee hee" "Shut Up!" past us . . . past us . . . and then . . . it stops.
The truck stopped.
And so did all our hearts.
The twins were not laughing now. The twins were not breathing.
Silent.
Dark.
The truck had definitely stopped. But why? We all sat there blinking . . . should we run? Stay still and hidden? Why had the truck stopped? Why was it so huge? Why—
Silent.
Dark.
Then CHUNK.
A truck door . . . opening.
Now our hearts doubly stopped.
Instinctively, as one body, we all turned to Sheila. And she knew what she had to do. She had to look.
Still silent.
Still dark.
She moved quietly, so so quietly to the eyehole in the card-

board wall. And she looked out at the truck. It was almost too dark to see anything, but the truck was a pickup truck. And old. And rusted. And BIG. The biggest truck she'd ever seen.

And the door was open.

And someone was getting out.

One foot went crunch on gravel and dirt. And then the other. Crunch. And she stared. She wasn't breathing, she needed every single ounce of her life to see in the dark, see who was coming. And she did see. Someone was walking from the truck . . . back toward the fortress.

Right toward us.

Except it wasn't a someone.

It wasn't even human.

GOD IN BED
Glenn Alterman

Dramatic
MAUREEN, 12

MAUREEN's *mother has left to gone to Rome to be at the pope's funeral.*

MAUREEN   Momma's gone. She left; went to see the pope. He died; and momma went to Rome, Italy, to be with him. Momma, she just loved the pope. Was always talking about him, all the time. He came to this town once, yeah, he did. Came to visit our church when Momma was just a girl. And he let Momma sit on his lap, she said. And Momma said that's when she had like a moment of divine inspiration. That's what she called it—"divine inspiration." I don't know what that means, but Momma says it changed her life forever. Can you imagine? Think that's why Momma made us all go to church every Sunday. And why we had to say grace before every meal, even breakfast, yeah. Momma really loved the pope. Loved him even more than Pappa I think. I think that's what made Pappa seem so jealous all the time. When she'd start going on about the pope, Pappa would like storm out of the room . . . Momma was cryin' real bad when she left. Said she didn't know if she'd ever be back. Said she had to go do God's work in Rome with the new pope. Then she gave me a big hug and then gave me her special rosary beads. Pappa said we're to pretend she's dead. Yeah, that's what he said, "dead." And he said we don't have to go to church or say grace before every meal anymore if we don't want to. God, I miss Momma—I miss her so much.

HERO

David L. Epstein

Dramatic
JACOB, 14

JACOB *spends too much time surfing the Internet for the next popular first-person shooter, when he comes across something he didn't expect.*

JACOB I spend days on my computer infiltrating imaginary compounds and taking out cliché terrorist targets. Geez, I've done it for years. And today, today I saw something I don't ever want to see again. I didn't even mean for it to happen. I mean, I thought it would be cool. I don't know what I thought. I know the parental codes my parents use and wanted to see what happened to that guy. The news won't shut up about it, and I wanted to know what it looked like. And now . . . I can't get the image out of my mind. Just sitting there on his knees in that desolate place. That orange jumpsuit. And the masked man next to him. So calm. He's so calm, it's scary. He knows what's about to happen. But the guy in orange doesn't know. He's been brought out there every single day and held in this same spot on his knees. They would tell him he was going to die and every day they would hold a knife to his neck and trick him. Mock execution. But not this time. This time they took the next step. The final step. He takes the knife and . . . Like it's nothing . . . And I watched it. And I thought . . . I thought it would be a movie . . . But it's real . . . it's real and terrible. It's the most awful thing I've ever seen. I wish I never was so stupid. I wish all these years I wasn't running around in imaginary worlds shooting up compounds and pretending to be a hero. I don't think I'll ever be able to play another computer game again after that. I just want to read a book. I want to read a book about something nice. About some place peaceful. But I don't know. Do books like that even exist? Will that help me get rid of what I've seen? Will it ever go away?

I HATE MATH
Connie Schindewolf

Comic
BOY, 12

A seventh-grade boy explains to his advisor why he hates math class.

BOY   I hate math! No, I mean I really hate math! The class that is . . . seventh-grade regular math. Huh, there's nothing regular about it. It's the most irregular class you could ever imagine . . . for dummies. Actually I'm not a dummy. I'm gifted in language arts. I think it's cuz my parents taught me to read at like two . . . yeah, that's right—two! They put those little magnetic letters on the fridge and taught me to read my name before I could walk. If they only would have started on the math a little earlier. I mean I think I've just convinced myself I suck at it . . . cuz I'm not stupid, really. But now I'm doomed . . . no chance of ever getting into advanced math now or in high school. As easy as it is, I'm still getting Cs and Ds cuz nothing goes on in there, except these lowlifes tearing the place up. I mean it. The poor teacher's been through like fifteen pencil sharpeners. When we're supposed to be dividing fractions, these future inmates are breaking their lead on purpose, so they can get out of their seats and cause a commotion. I mean nothing gets done. If she doesn't hear a swearword all period, we get a piece of candy. Can you believe it? I get sick to my stomach just walking to math class cuz I know what's coming. I just sit there and never say anything. One time I gave one of the kids a dirty look when he threw something at the teacher, and he said to me, "Your sister's real cute. And I know where you live." So, I just sit there and never say anything and watch the poor teacher with her tons of paperwork and stacks of office referrals, which never do any good anyway. God, I hate math!

I THINK I LOVE YOU
Sharon Goldner

Comic
SIBOBAN, 12

SIBOBAN, *a precocious girl, tells us about how she came to love David Cassidy, the teen idol from* The Partridge Family.

SIBOBAN   I'm in love. You probably don't think anything of it because I'm just a kid and you wonder, just how real can it be, that I've got so much more living to do, but that just means you're old and you've forgotten. I will never forget what it's like to be a kid when I grow up. That's the problem with adults. The dementia doesn't start when you're ancient; it starts as soon as you're not a kid anymore. [*Pause.*] At first I was in love with Jack Wild. He's that English actor who was Academy Award–nominated for *Oliver*. I didn't love him then; I didn't even know him then. But after that, he was on *Pufnstuf*. He was this kid named Jimmy who had a golden flute, and he lands in this place called Living Island where everything is alive the way humans are—like the trees even talk. It's all one great big trippy place, and the evil witch, Witchiepoo, wants that golden flute. In every episode, she concocts some crazy plan to get it, and Jimmy and Pufnstuf, the dragon mayor of Living Island, foil her plans. My friend Michelle and I were in love with Jack Wild. You can call it a crush, and maybe it looks that way to adults, but it shouldn't be that easily dismissed. Our loves flatten us out just the same as yours do you. So one day I'm grooving on Jack Wild and Michelle comes over and says, "We love *him* now," and she smacks down a teen magazine folded to a picture of David Cassidy. It was before *The Partridge Family* even aired their first episode.

So, I look at him and he's okay and all, but I say to Michelle, "What about Jack?" and she says, "We don't like him anymore." Now, before you consider me a follower, I've got to say that Michelle comes with some pretty good credentials: she may be a whole year younger than me, but she's the youngest of four sisters and she's got boobs already. I'm not talking your beginning double As, mind you—I am talking down-the-alphabet cups, like a D. I'm not jealous. My day will come, I mean, everyone gets boobs, don't they? There are even a few male teachers at school with what look like boobs. So I'm just waiting for mine.

I THINK I LOVE YOU
Sharon Goldner

Comic
SIBOBAN, 12

SIBOBAN *is in love with teen idol David Cassidy of* The Partridge Family. *She has a poster of him on her bedroom wall. David has stepped out of the poster and* SIBOBAN *tells him about how she still loves him, even though the other kids have moved on.*

SIBOBAN   Michelle likes Mickey Abramovitz now. What, you haven't heard of Mickey A? That's what she calls him. You haven't heard of him because he's nobody you would have ever heard of. Mickey A's just a boy at school. Michelle has moved on from the glossy pages of *Tiger Beat* and *16 Magazine* to the high-end gloss of oily skin, pimples, poor attempts at shaving, and Adam's apples that should really be called Adam's nuts because the voices they produce crack so much. [*Pause.*] I meant nuts like peanuts. Not, you know, the other kind. That's what the boys call their, you know, down-there place. So Michelle is with Mickey A now. She gave me all of her David Cassidy posters and magazines. I didn't understand why she can't like them both, and she said, "This is not Utah, Siboban." I realize that, of course. Because of Donny Osmond. He's in the teen magazines, too. He's a Mormon, but he only has one mother and father. He's not my type. Too goody-two-shoes. I tried to get Michelle back on board, but she wasn't interested. She and Mickey A got all the way to second base recently. I wasn't sure what that was exactly—I mean, I always strike out when we play softball in gym. I've never made it even to first base. But then, Michelle cleared that up for me, and I realized I've never made it to first base that way either. They stuck their tongues in each other's mouths. Gross! I can't imagine doing that. I had to rethink all of those romantic kisses on my mother's soap operas once I knew what they were doing inside their mouths. Michelle says that's why you close your eyes when you're doing it, so you don't have to think about it.

I'M THIRTEEEN
Paul Barile

Comic
A KID, 13

In this play, a KID (who may be played by either a male or female actor) is addressing the audience directly

KID   It isn't always easy being thirteen. When you're a little kid, people expect you to paint rainbows and play in puddles and say really cute things. When you're a teenager, they expect you to keep an eye on the little kids. Parents always say things like, "You're old enough to know better." If they have to point it out like that—then maybe you're not. Parents are interesting: on the one hand, they tell you to not grow up too fast; on the other hand, they want you grown enough to help with the chores. When you're thirteen, you're at the prime age for chores. You can't get out of them—even if you do know better.

A lot of adults think that all kids are exactly the same. They think we all like the same things. They think we all *don't* like the same things. We do like a lot of the same things—but the big question that a lot of adults forget to ask is *why* we like these things. We don't always like them for the same reasons. We like them for our own reasons. We are individuals. Each kid is an individual with the potential to do a lot of different things. We are not defined by our age or by our culture—not even by our family or our neighborhood. We are defined by who we are. The future is unlimited for every kid who understands that.

You might want to horrify your family and become an

actor. You might want to be something more stable like a businessperson or a teacher. Maybe you'll choose a noble career where you help people. Maybe you just want a nice quiet existence with a family and a job and a garden. Whatever choice you make—you have to believe that you are unique. You are a very special individual—one of a kind. Then you have to make the adults around you realize that, too. You have to be patient. This may take some time. Parents don't come with an owner's manual.

IN THE FOREST OF GONE
Don Nigro

Dramatic
LORRY, 12

In the attic of her Aunt Moll's house, LORRY REEDY, *age 12—a smart, funny, stubborn girl—is hiding out with a copy of an old novel about the ancient Lemurians, which describes the mysterious continent of Gondwananland. She and her sister and brother have been abandoned once again by their mother, and* Lorry *is very upset. She is worried that her mother is insane and that she herself will also be insane, and never be able to love and be loved in a normal way. Her sister, June, 13, has been trying to comfort her by telling her that she's not crazy and that their mother will come back again soon, as she always does. But* Lorry *isn't buying it.*

LORRY   Sometimes I come up here and I'm scared to look in that old mirror because I'm afraid I'll look in there and there won't be anybody looking back at me. In this book, in Gondwanaland, there's a forest, called the Forest of Gone. And in the Forest of Gone, everybody who ever went away from you is there. You go into that forest and they're all there, all the ones who abandoned you, that you thought you were never going to see again. And at first you're so happy to see them, and you want to talk to them and ask them why they went away from you, what they were thinking or what you did wrong. But they won't look at you. They just look right through you. And you realize they're looking at somebody else. Somebody behind you that you can't see. I don't want her to come back. Because if she comes back she's just going to leave again. She comes back and she gets you to like her again and then just when you start to trust her she goes away again, and she keeps doing it over and over again until she's made you as crazy as she is. So don't try and tell me it's going to be all right, because it's not all right and it's never going to be all right—because I'm crazy like she is, and I'm going to grow up and betray the people who love me and run away from everybody who cares about me, and I'll end up in the Forest of Gone. And you'll come to see me there, and I'll just look right through you. I'll just look right through you. Because I'll really be looking at somebody who isn't there. Because the person we love is always the person who isn't there. That's how we know they're the person we love. Because they're not there.

IN THE PICTURE

John Levine

Comic
IAN, 13

IAN *is alone in his room, rehearsing his bar mitzvah speech. He addresses the audience.*

IAN [*Practicing, trying out various lines.*] Ladies and gentlemen, Mom, Rabbi, members of the congregation . . . Today I am a man! [*Pause.*] No. . . . Hi everybody!

[*Like a blues singer:*]

I'm a maaaan! Uh-uh. [*Pause.*] We're gathered here today to . . . I'll come back to that part . . . Wait, I've got it. . . . Call me Ishmael. I'd like to use this opportunity to invite you to join me in thinking about a story—a Bible story—the story of Abraham and Sarah and Hagar and Ishmael. Do you remember that story? No? Let me refresh your memory. First, there's Sarah. Sarah was married to Abraham and she had trouble getting pregnant. She finally did get pregnant, and this was pre-IVF and all that, don't forget. And she named her baby Isaac, which means "I laughed," because when God told her she was finally going to have a baby, that's what she did—she laughed, because she was way past the childbearing years, even by today's standards. But let's back up a little. Before she had Isaac, Sarah had pretty much given up on the whole idea of being a mom, and, figuring this was unfair to her husband, she arranged for Abraham to do the nasty with her servant, a much younger woman, whose name was Hagar. And sure enough, Abraham gets together with Hagar and bing-bing, nine months later Hagar has a baby. And she names their son Ishmael. So, just to recap: Abraham gets his son, Sarah doesn't have to feel guilty about her husband not having a kid, and Hagar, well, not much changes for Hagar—she's still a servant. But what about Ishmael? Where does he fit into the family picture? Okay, back to Sarah. Like I said, she ends up having her own baby with Abraham, so at this point she could feel complete because she has her own biological child. We have a family unit now: Abraham and Sarah and Isaac. But what about Ishmael? Sarah, who, for the most part, is a pretty nice old lady, decides that Ishmael is a bad influence on Isaac, so she tells Abraham to get rid of Hagar and Ishmael and even though he doesn't like the idea, Abraham says adios to Hagar and sends her out into the desert. As the story goes, God eventually steps in and rescues the wandering mother and child and even gives Ishmael his own place in history. But we seem to overlook these very important facts: that Abraham was the first deadbeat dad, Hagar was the first single mom, and Ishmael was . . . Was what? Now I know this speech is supposed to be inspiring and hopeful and full of great sound bites for the video memories, but I need to figure this stuff out. Because, because today I am a Man. So if anybody out there knows, if anybody in this congregation can clue me in on what Ishmael did to deserve not having a father around, I'd be really, really grateful. Thank you for listening.

JUDY MACCABEE

Susan Horowitz

Comic
JUDY, 10 to 12

JUDY *wakes up in Jerusalem, 165 BCE—the time of the Maccabees, and the origin of Hanukkah. She speaks to Teddly, her teddy bear.*

JUDY   What do you want, Teddly Bear? . . . You're always hungry . . . Stop poking me! . . . Cut it out! . . . I was up all night worrying about Papa! He promised to come back. But where is he? . . . Okay, I know you can't talk, so act out the words . . . You're tugging at your ear . . .

[*She tugs her ear.*]

   . . . which means . . . it sounds like something. Okay, what does it sound like? . . . You're licking your lips . . .

[*She licks her lips.*]

   . . . it sounds like . . .

[*She pretends to taste something delicious.*]

   Honey! . . . What word sounds like "honey"? . . . "Bunny"? . . . "Sunny"? . . . No? . . . You're rubbing your paws together . . .

[*She rubs her hands together.*]

   Money? . . . Money! . . . Which means . . .

[*She looks at the audience, delighted.*]

   Customers! We're open! Don't go anywhere!

[*She does a rhyming sales pitch to the audience.*]

   Mezuzahs and menorahs, and music for your horas. And lotsa matzah, Lord be praised, and calendars for holidays.

From Purim to Passover, step right up and look them over.
Our business is straight cash. We got idols—I mean bot-
tles—here to smash! And now for somethin' finger lickin',
try my crispy kosher chicken! Papa usually does the cooking, but now that he's in the Maccabee army . . . well I'm
doing the best I can. I'm sure my customers . . . my hungry
customers . . .

[*To the audience:*]

. . . that means you! Don't pay any attention to Teddly. He's
just a bear, what does he know about cooking?
What? You don't like my chicken? . . . You're not hungry?

[*She is momentarily downcast, but quickly recovers.*]

I know! You want fashion! Designer labels at dis-
count prices! Our rags—I mean our designer fash-
ions—are imported from . . . uh . . . everywhere!

KEY LIME MOON WITH VENUS RISING
Mark Lambeck

Comic
ETHEL MAE, 15

The play is set in the late 1990s, when ETHEL MAE is around 60 years old. This monologue is a flashback to her youth and takes place around 1950. In this scene, ETHEL MAE is seated at a student desk in a high school classroom in McComas, West Virginia.

ETHEL MAE   Well, well. Will you lookee here, Charisse. An A-plus. Can you believe it? I, Ethel Mae Donner, has actually gotten herself an A-plus on a creative writin' assignment. Huh?

[*She listens.*]

　　Watcha talkin' about? I most certainly did.

[*Holds out the paper.*]

　　See for y'self. There it is, "A+" in big red letters. And ya see that re-mark she made in the margin, "Very imaginative. An extremely creative work." I knew I could do this creative-style writin' if I set my mind to it.

[*Looks up suddenly.*]

　　Huh? Oh, excuse me, ma'am. Nothin' really. I was just showin' Charisse my paper. You what? [*Surprised.*] You were? You mean, here . . . out loud? In front of the whole class? Well, that's very nice of you, ma'am. I don't mean no disrespec' but I don't think I can . . . No. It's just that readin' out loud . . . it's embarrassin', ya know? I don't think I . . . Yes ma'am.

[*Stands up, holding the paper. She looks around sheepishly, then reads.*]

"My Life as a Venusian," by Ethel Mae Donner. My name is Vista. And my work is light. I spread light with the wand I carry everywhere I go. Because light is bright and cheerful. It makes people see things they can't always see. People are happy when I show them my light. The nights here are long. So my light is important to the people here on Venus. We live a peaceful life. Those stories you read in them astronomical-type books about Venus being fiery and hot and red? Well, they's just not so, is all. Them books make out our beautiful planet to be something more like hell set in the sky. But it's not true! It in't hell at all.

On Venus, there is no poverty. Clover grows wild and it's there for the pickin'. Venusian clover is magical. You can make it taste like anything you like—cherries or watermelon, sweet potato pie or homemade ice cream.

Except for the long nights during the dark season, the weather is always fine. Flowers grow everywhere. Beautiful gardens jus' spring up over hills and in clearings. There are fields of violets and gardenias. People don't argue 'bout things like neighbors' cars with rusty mufflers waking up the whole neighborhood.

There are no hospitals. People don't get sick here. There are no police or firemen neither 'cause we have no crimes or fires. We have learned our lesson from the goddess whose name we borrowed for our planet. Our mission is to spread her word: "love." That's the word. It means cooperation and carin' about fellow Venusians. Some build simple shelters. Some plant seeds from which our sweet clover grows and spreads wild.

And I do my part. I bring the light. Waving my wand to deliver it to those whose lives need a little brightening. Golden rays shine down and attach themselves to mortals who absorb the light and learn to glow from within. I am Vista and I can bring you light, too. On a clear night, look up into the sky. If you look carefully, you'll see bright lines of red, yellow, and purple connecting some of the stars. That is the light of Vista. It reaches out to touch those mortals who need guidance. I bring rays of hope. It's there. You only need to know where to look.

LAESTRYGONIANS
Don Nigro

Seriocomic
JESSIE, 10

JESSIE ARMITAGE, age 10, lives in a big, falling-apart Gothic man-sion in a small town in East Ohio with her parents and sisters. She loves very much her older half brother John Rose, who has left home to become an actor with Andrew McDuffy's theater com-pany, which is now touring in Ireland. She misses John a lot, and writes him many letters about her life in Ohio. She is very smart, very independent, and always gets what she wants. She is a bit of a handful, but everybody in her family loves her. This is her first letter to John. It is spoken by the actress as if she is talking to him, and we, the audience, are standing in for him. She does not actu-ally write while she speaks. Molly is her older sister. John L. Sullivan was a famous prizefighter. Theodore Roosevelt, president from 1901 to 1909, was known for his feisty attitude, spectacles, large mustache, and big teeth. Armitage is also the name of the town she lives in.

JESSIE February 13th, 1912. Wet, dreary Armitage. Dear Johnny. You are very bad and never answer my letters except once every five or six of them, shame on you. I am ten years old now and I require letters. I keep yours in a little drawer by my bed and hide them from Molly, who is very stupid and jealous because you don't write to her, which is silly because she never writes to you, but Molly is a silly person and wants everything for free and is pouty and foul-tempered and the cat had five little kittens, one with a black eye I named John L. Sullivan, although she is a girl, I think, and three have boots. Where in Ireland are you? Tell me so I can color you on the map. Papa is cross when I color in his books, but I tell him I've got to follow Johnny and Mr. McDuffy through Ireland or they'll get lost, and Papa growls like he always does and then lets me up on his lap and we follow along in the book. There is a kitten on my head now, not John L. Sullivan, and I wish I could send him to you in the mail but I worry because he doesn't speak Irish and might get beat up by the Irish cats so I have named him Theodore Roosevelt. Johnny I miss you bunches and love you very much and excuse this mark on the paper, Theodore Roosevelt threw up. Always, always, your loving sister, Jessie. P.S. Be my Valentine, you promised.

LAESTRYGONIANS
Don Nigro

Seriocomic
JESSIE, 11

JESSIE ARMITAGE, age 11, lives in a big, falling-apart Gothic man-sion in a small town in East Ohio with her parents and sisters. She loves very much her older half brother John Rose, who has left home to become an actor with Andrew McDuffy's theater com-pany. She misses John a lot, and writes him many letters about her life in Ohio. She is very smart, very independent, and always gets what she wants. She is a bit of a handful, but everybody in her fam-ily loves her. This is her speaking her letter to us, the audience, as if she is talking to him. She does not actually write while she speaks. Lizzy, Dorothy, and Molly are her older sisters. Dorothy has been deaf and unable to speak clearly since contracting scarlet fever as a child. When Jessie says "preconscious," she means "precocious."

JESSIE   June 27th, 1913. Dear Johnny. It's very hot today, and
there's a thunderstorm coming, which I love, although
everybody thinks I'm crazy, and Mother is afraid of storms,
but sometimes I sneak out and let it rain on me until I'm
soaked. When Lizzy catches me she scolds me like the
dickens and tells me I'll get pneumonia, but I just giggle at
her and pretty soon she starts giggling, too. Lizzy has a nice
laugh when she isn't trying to act like an old lady. I don't
know why she does that. I'm eleven and I act more like I'm
eighteen than she does. Mother says I'm very preconscious,
but I think I'm as conscious as the next person. She is well
and sends her love, but she and Papa barely speak to each
other. Honestly, they're so grumpy sometimes. What's
wrong with them? And Molly keeps snipping at me, but
Dorothy is my best friend because I blurt out all the things

she'd say if she could talk. We all miss you very much. I still remember the night you left, but I wish I had a picture of you now, as that was many years ago when I was just a tiny little innocent child of six. Now I'm almost grown up and you're playing beggars and dead bodies and crazy people. I loved your story about how the cow kept mooing in the field while poor Mr. McDuffy was trying to be King Lear. I'm reading all the plays you're in. Molly says I just pretend to understand them, so I acted Juliet's whole death scene for her and I was so good she cried. Molly is such a powder. I love her a lot. She's very pretty and boys like her. Boys don't chase Lizzy much. I don't know why. Personally, I think boys are stupid and should be locked up until they're old like Papa. Please come home and visit us soon and don't forget me and send me your picture. Love, Jessie.

LAESTRYGONIANS
Don Nigro

Seriocomic
JESSIE, 12

JESSIE ARMITAGE, *age 12, lives in a big, falling-apart Gothic mansion in a small town in East Ohio with her parents and sisters. She loves very much her older half brother John Rose, who has left home to become an actor with Andrew McDuffy's theater company. She misses John a lot, and writes him many letters about her life in Ohio. She is very smart, very independent, and always gets what she wants. She is a bit of a handful, but everybody in her family loves her. In this monologue,* JESSIE *is speaking her letter to us, the audience, as if she is talking to John. She does not actually write while she speaks. Lizzy and Molly are her older sisters. Sarah is their bossy but much-loved housekeeper. The reason there is tension between Papa and Mama over Uncle Rhys is that he is in fact the real father of both* JESSIE *and John, although Jessie doesn't know that yet. Jessie's childhood crush on her brother is becoming deeper and more serious as she gets older. It will eventually destroy her.*

JESSIE   January 6th, 1914. Dear Johnny. It was so wonderful to get your letter with the pictures and newspaper clippings. You look just like I remember only better, and seeing your name in the papers really impressed everybody around here, even Papa, who is not too well. I wish he'd let Mother take care of him. What's wrong between Mother and Father? It seems to have something to do with Uncle Rhys, but I don't know what, and nobody will talk about it. If you know, I wish you'd tell me. It's never been so cold since the beginning of the world. We went ice-skating and Molly and Cletis were showing off. Cletis is a goon and keeps trying to kiss me when Molly isn't looking. I tell him I'm only twelve but he says I'm developed for my age. Molly sees a lot of boys but always comes back to Cletis. I guess some people are just made for each other in a horrible sort of way. But the next time Clete Rainey tries to lay a smooch on me, I'm going to punch him right in the nose. We had a beautiful Christmas, and I wished so bad you'd surprise us and come home. I kept imagining how you'd show up on the porch on Christmas Eve and we could feed you turkey and hot punch and sit in front of the fire and you could tell me all about Scotland and Wales and all the places you've been with Mr. McDuffy. His daughter Marina is very beautiful in this picture. Is she your girlfriend? Because if she is, I'm going to have to come over there and punch her in the nose, too. Now I've got to go because Sarah and Lizzy are having a fit because I didn't help them with the wash, but it wasn't my fault, I was watching snow blow off the pine trees and it was so beautiful I couldn't get away. Please come back soon and try not to forget me. Love, Jessie.

THE LAST WISH
John Yearley

Seriocomic
EUGENE, 12

EUGENE *is talking to his friends Anna and JJ. The three friends
have a lamp that they think might be magic. They have squan-
dered the first two wishes and are deciding what to do with the
third.* EUGENE *is thinking about using the third wish to keep his
mother from marrying her boyfriend, Todd.*

EUGENE   The weirdest thing just happened. I was sitting in
my room, wondering what I was going to do, when I heard
Todd outside. He was clipping the hedges! Right outside
my window! I was so mad I grabbed the magic lamp and
wished that Todd would go away. I know I shouldn't have,
but I was so mad! Guess what—nothing happened. He just
kept clipping away. Clip clip clip. Clip clip clip. I was really
starting to lose it, when I heard this weird sound coming from the kitchen. I couldn't figure out what it was, so
I went to go look. It was my mom. She was whistling. See,
my mom is a *great* whistler, but she hasn't whistled in so
long I forgot. I just sat there and watched her skip around
the kitchen, whistling, making dinner. I thought, you know,
she's *happy*. I think it's because of Todd. It must be. And
that made me feel really bad about my wish. But just when
I thought that, my mom looked right at me. It was weird,
like she could read my mind or something. She called me
over and said that she knew that this change was really
hard, and that she was really proud of how well I was doing.
And then she said that she knew that Todd tried too hard
and drove me nuts. She said Todd never had kids and he really liked me and wanted me to like him. And then she did

the *weirdest* thing. She asked for my help! She asked me if I could help make Todd feel okay in our house. She said she would be really grateful to me if I could do that. "Grateful?" Can you believe that?

THE LATE BUS
Peter Mercurio

Dramatic
ANDREW, 14

ANDREW *is speaking with a guidance counselor after witnessing another kid get bullied.*

ANDREW There was this kid who I went to middle school with. Kenny Fitzpatrick. Sort of a geek. He got teased all the time. I sat behind him in English class. Whenever Mrs. Langer had her back turned, all these wet, wadded-up spitballs came flying right in front of me, most of them hitting their target. Kenny. He'd turn red and scream, "Stop it!" That only made the rest of the class laugh. Mrs. Langer would scowl and say, "Let's behave now, class." Her standard response. And things would settle down, until the next time. Me, my standard response was, well, it was actually no response at all. After school one day, I saw Kenny waiting for the late bus. All the jocks took it after practice. You can imagine the scene. Kenny, me, and a bunch of jocks. You'd think the blockheads had just won the Super Bowl, the way they acted when they saw Kenny. "Faggot!" one shouted. Then the onslaught began. You see, if one starts it, they all have to join in—otherwise, they'd be one themselves. That's how it worked. Somehow, I always escaped. Maybe I was invisible. Better Kenny than me, I guess. "What's a little girl like you doing here all by yourself?" Nope, they didn't see me. Kenny didn't answer. He squirmed away. They followed. "You think you're getting on this bus?" "What's a matter? Huh?" For once, why couldn't the late bus be early? The driver would never have allowed the abuse to continue. Finally, the bus pulled up from around the corner. I glanced over. They had taken Kenny's glasses off. Two took turns poking at him. He stumbled. "What's the matter, you blind or something?" "Shut Up!" Kenny screamed. "What did you say?" "Leave me alone." "No, I think you said 'shut up.' Guys, isn't that what he said?" "Kick his ass," someone else yelled. The rest happened in slow motion. One last shove and Kenny tripped off the curb. The late bus rolled over and crushed both of his legs. I'll never forget the crunch. The driver jumped out of the bus and dragged him back to the sidewalk. That's when Kenny saw me. He just stared. "Why didn't you help me?" he asked. I just stared back. I couldn't answer. All I know is I don't want to be invisible anymore.

LE MORTE D'ALEX

Brandon M. Crose

Seriocomic
Alex, 10 to 15

ALEX *(who can be played as either a male or female character) reads a report in class.*

ALEX   "Evolution," by Alex Cademon. Once the Earth was not called "Earth"—it was not called anything, because there was no one around to call it anything. The only things that were around were one-celled organisms called "amoeba," and they were not capable of speech. So there was no school, either. Or church, or anything else that was stupid and boring.

[*Turns a page, gaining confidence.*]

But I guess there were no books either, or uncles who would read bedtime stories when you went to live with him after your parents died in a SUV rollover accident, so these one-celled gooey things evolved (which means to "develop") into things like jellyfish and worms and stuff. And they became things like turtles and dinosaurs, then primates, then cavemen and cavewomen. Charles Darwin was a man who thought that humans evolved from monkeys, and I think that he was probably right, judging from most of you.

[*Turns another page, confident now.*]

But here is what I think. Mr. Gibbons says that energy must come from energy, and life is energy, which means that amoebas came from pure energy, which only could have come from an exploding star, which turned into amoebas, which turned into us a long time later. So we all have the energy of the universe within us, which is why people should not treat other people badly just because they are different.

[*No longer reading.*]

A lot of genius people were different people before they were famous, and lots of genius people do not ever become famous people, because maybe their differences were too different and everyone thought they were just weird. But what I think is that genius people are evolved from you average people, and you are just too primitive to understand that. Thank you.

THE LEGEND OF WENCESLAS
Walt Vail

Dramatic
KARELA, 10

KARELA *is speaking to a member of the Czech Underground about a possible opportunity for children to escape from German-occupied Czechoslovakia in World War II.*

KARELA   Do you know my mama? She's a crazy lady! She has a bad temper, and she never stops talking. When I woke up one morning last week, I heard Mama talking to the kitchen door. She does that a lot, but this time she wanted the door to answer a question. "Will you open?" She kept asking, "Will you open?" But the door wouldn't answer her, so she got so mad and she kicked it, and it still wouldn't open, and she broke her foot—her big toe, I think. Oh, she yelled like a train whistle, and her foot swelled up, and now she has to walk with a crutch. She won't go to the doctor, she says no one can fix a broken toe. She thinks she knows more than any doctor, and I believe her, because she knows everything. If I pick my nose, or forget to wash my face, she knows it. She knows it without even looking at me—I don't know how she does that. She's amazing! One Sunday I went exploring Prague with my friend Jiri, who lives across the street—we were supposed to go to church, but we went exploring instead. Jiri is a boy of great imagination! I really like him, and when I grow up—I'm ten now, same age as Jiri—I'm going to marry Jiri. No question, my mind's made up! Anyway, when I got home, I told Mama everything the Priest said—he always says the same thing every Sunday—and I named every hymn we sang, and even offered to sing one for her, but Mama knew I wasn't in church, and she knew I crossed Charles Bridge, and she even knew I went to Tyn Church Square! She's amazing! How does she know everything? She won't tell me, but someday I'll find out the secret, and I'll become a person who knows everything, too! I love Mama. She's a very brave Czech lady—the bravest in Prague! Yesterday a German soldier came to our front door to complain that she not only won't stop talking, but she insists on speaking Czech. He said, "Speak all you want, but do it in German!" She bounced right at him on one foot, and hit him with her crutch, and chased him off the front steps! I think he yelled something bad at her in German, and she yelled right back in Czech. And when you've been yelled at by Mama, you've been yelled at! Wait a minute, I think I hear Mama calling me. Sorry, I must go! Never keep Mama waiting! And, oh, yes—when we escape from Prague, will Mama be going with us? 'Cause I can't escape without Mama.

I love her, and I could never leave her alone in Prague.

THE LEGEND OF WENCESLAS
Walt Vail

Dramatic
FRANTA, 11

World War II, during the German occupation of Czechoslovakia.
FRANTA identifies herself to a Czech Underground messenger from
her imprisoned father. The Underground messenger will, later, give
her a message about escaping over the border to Switzerland with
her father and two brothers.

FRANTA   I'm Franta, and I'm eleven years and one month old,
and I live in Prague with my brothers Jiri, age ten, and Gus-
tav, age thirteen. I've had to grow up too quickly, and I have
a feeling I've missed my childhood. Things happen when
your country is invaded by Germans. It can't be helped—
but never mind. Mama went to visit some relatives in
Switzerland, and left us with Papa—but then the soldiers
came in the night and arrested Papa for being an editor of
a newspaper. The Germans don't want us to read, write, or
speak in Czech—they say we were once Germans, and we
must speak German. Ha! We were never German! I miss my
mama—her warm hugs and her wonderful cooking! Now
I have to feed my brothers on dried potato meal, and it
tastes like the Germans have mixed sawdust into it. Mama
is probably eating chocolate in Switzerland—she can't get
back to Prague, and she can't send us any chocolate, because the Germans will open packages and eat everything
themselves. Unbelievable! It's not enough for them to take
over our country—they must eat our chocolate, too. But
at least we have dried potato meal—poor Papa is probably starving in that camp they sent him to. I'm so worried
about him! But I must be strong, and not worry my broth-

ers. Mama would want me to be strong. I must act very grown up, and pretend that everything will be all right. And it will be. No, I don't believe that our ancient King Wenceslas will come to life after five hundred years, and bring his famous sword, and slay all the Germans. I don't believe in legends. And I don't want the Germans to be slain—I just want them to go home to Berlin or Hamburg, or wherever they came from, and leave us Czechs alone. And free Papa from prison, and let Mama come home to Prague. We Czechs are a freedom-loving people—and we can't be held prisoner for very long. Better days will come—until then, I'll be strong. Now, tell me everything you know about my papa. Is he well? Is he hungry?

LITTLE MR. WONDERFUL
Ben Clossey and Carolyn Boriss-Krimsky

Comic
JESSE, 13

JESSE has a little brother, Dylan, age 3. JESSE's at a party with a bunch of kids from middle school. He doesn't know all of them that well, but wants to. They're talking about family weirdness and annoying siblings.

JESSE   My little brother is apparently King of the World—at least in our house. Okay, he's three and I'm thirteen, but still. He's considered an adorable toddler, and I'm just a teen with problems . . . lots of problems. No matter what he does, he rocks my parents' world. But he drives me crazy. Last week, he poured glue on my iPad, and spilled chocolate syrup on my new sweatshirt. And that's for starters! He gets everything he wants. We practically had to hire a moving van last Christmas to get all his gifts back from our grandparents' house. The only thing I got from them was a dictionary! Can you believe that? A dictionary! They're like clueless. I mean, Wikipedia anyone? Hello? No one uses a dictionary anymore! The truth is, the only attention I get is when I do something wrong. And since I'm grounded almost every weekend, I guess I do lots of things wrong. I watch Little Mr. Wonderful get all his needs met by everyone, including me. My parents keep telling me to be nice to him, and give him whatever he wants, or else . . . or else what? I get grounded! As soon as I give him water, he says, "Milk now," and then I dump out the water, and refill the cup with milk. Then I come back with milk and he says he wants water instead! It never ends until he's satisfied or too tired to bug me. But, you know, the other day I was thinking. What if I could get this little twerp to do something for *me*? YES! But what? The weird thing was . . . it happened by accident. I came home with a failing grade on my French test . . . Yeah, again . . . Okay, so it was a D. How did I get a D? That's another story. Anyway, naturally I didn't want my parents to see it. So I shoved it in my backpack, and some-how, the King of the Castle was looking for drawing paper and got into my stuff. And get this. Before I knew it, little Miracle Man was scribbling all over my big fat D with his magic markers—drawing all over it! AWESOME! He saved me, he actually saved me! From now on, I'll give him all my tests with bad grades and let him create art projects out of them. You know, I might even start calling him my Little Picasso. What do you think?

THE MAD GENIUS OF SHUFFLEBURY CENTRAL SCHOOL
Luc Reid

Comic
MARTA, 8 to 12

MARTA SPROING *is a brilliant inventor who's so preoccupied with science that she sometimes loses track of things like safety and fairness. In this scene, her science-fair project has ended in tragedy when a rocket she designed blows up with (she believes) the class guinea pig on it. Marta attends a school assembly the next day where she's sure she's going to get suspended, or worse. At the opening of the assembly, the principal takes her aside and she makes an impassioned speech in hopes of winning a little more support before the axe falls.*

MARTA   Ms. Principal, teachers, staff, fellow students . . . I come before you today humbled and also saddened. It's true that Mrs. McPickles the Guinea Pig was destined for greatness. It's true that Mrs. McPickles had the heart of an adventurer, that she yearned for the unexplored vastness of space. It's also true that my guinea pig rocket was a groundbreaking invention that staggers the mind with its genius. Yet . . . should I have been experimenting with nuclear fusion in the cafeteria during recess? Should I have endangered the life of this brave guinea pig and the lives of . . . perhaps . . . lots of students . . . with my amazingly brilliant experiment? Possibly not. But I ask you to see this sorrowful moment for what it is, a daring leap in scientific progress. Are such leaps safe? Of course not. Where would the Wright Brothers be if they hadn't crashed so many prototypes into the cruel sands of Kitty Hawk? Where would Jonas Salk be if he'd limited his imagination and cured, not polio, but toenail fungus? Actually, I guess he'd be really rich. But where would Marie Curie be if she hadn't poisoned herself with radioactivity? Maybe those aren't great examples. The point is that Project Space Squeaky is science, and you can't argue with science. Everybody knows that! If you stand in the way of science, science will just run you over like a big submarine on wheeled tracks . . . not that I'm threatening to run you over. Although wow, a submarine on wheeled tracks would be really cool. Think of it this way: by punishing the well-meaning, or at least mostly polite scientist (me) who almost helped Mrs. McPickles travel to the very stars, you stomp all over the greatness of Mrs. McPickles' grand gesture, her heroic flight to altitudes attained—even with the, uh . . . technical problems—by very few guinea pigs! By punishing me, you soil the memory of this singular rodent, this sweet little explorer, this . . .

[*She begins to get a little teary-eyed.*]

   . . . fluffy little ball of bravery . . . this . . . this . . .

[MARTA *breaks down in sobs.*]

   Mrs. McPickles!

MADISON

Deanna Alisa Ableser

Dramatic
MADISON, 12 to 14

MADISON *wears long dark clothes that cover up her arms and legs. She as been pulled out of class for "attitude issues." She is speaking to a school counselor.*

MADISON   You really think you're going to swoop in here and make things all okay, don't you? You have your stupid little degree in counseling and you're here to solve the problems of all the poor little teenage girls that go around and look all sad and everything, right? Is that what they told you in your fancy little counseling school? Go out and make a difference, right? Go out and fix the world's problems. You can do it. We believe in you. [*Beat.*] All right, go ahead. I'm here. I'm waiting . . . sitting here. Go on. [*Beat.*] What? You don't have the magic answer at your disposal? You can't immediately solve my horrible teenage angst? You mean I'm still going to be stuck in my stupid life, pissed off and angry at the world? Wow, what an amazing concept. I'm so thrilled that I'm sitting here wasting my time in your nicely designed office. Do I get the requisite candy now? Mmm . . . let's see. Oh no, I'd better be careful which candy I pick. You might go and get all psychoanalytical on me or something. What if I choose the one with peanuts? Oh no, what could that possibly mean? [*Beat.*] Not talking again? Really? Could I seriously have you that stumped? Great, the little psycho girl who cuts herself has the super amazing counselor all stumped? I'm good . . . I mean, really good. [*Beat.*] Okay, I've got you all figured out. You're just going to continue to sit there and look all smug and satisfied, like the poor girl's just going to spill her beans and you're going to end up as the hero. Yeah, that's your plan, right? Huh? [*Beat.*] Would you just fricking say something? [*Beat.*] Seriously, you're not a mute, are you? [*Beat.*] Look, I'm not playing this stupid game. Maybe other people will buy your moronic "I'm going to sit here and say nothing" game, but not me. No way. It's not going to work with me. I'm stronger than that. Much stronger . . . and if you think I'm going to break down and let you in . . . well then . . . [*Beat.*] Would you just say something? Anything? [*Beat.*] Look here, Mrs. "Super Counselor," I'm telling you I'm not liking this. I'm really not liking this. Could you just for once . . . [*Starts crying.*]

This is the ugliest office I have ever been in at this ugly place. You can't even make sure there's enough sunlight coming in through the windows. Couldn't the stupid school get some garish windows that frickin' let in the sun for once in a while? Maybe if there were some windows that let in the sun, there would be some small amount of hope for us "poor little teenage girls" that are forced to sit in here and blabber on like someone really actually cares about us.

MARGO MAINE DOESN'T LIVE HERE ANYMORE
Kayla Cagan

Dramatic
ANNIE, 12 to 15

ANNIE *tells her sister, Margo, why she shouldn't go to college out of state.*

ANNIE I know you're going away. And I'm really happy you got into Stanford. Mom said she knew the whole time that you were going to be accepted and Uncle Marshall and Aunt Barbara said they expected nothing less from you. [*Pause.*] But I did. [*Pause.*] I was secretly hoping you wouldn't get in, that somehow you'd flunk Latin or Calculus and then we could . . . you could . . . stay at Franklin High one more year. [*Pause.*] It's not that I don't want you to go off to school. I just don't understand why you have to move a whole state away. You've always been here. What if I need you? [*Pause.*] How am I going to know what to wear? I won't! Who's going to pick me up from parties? Not Mom and Dad! Who's going to help me sneak into R-rated movies? Nobody! You're the one with the fake ID! [*Pause.*] I don't care if I can have your room. I don't care if I can use the computer all the time now. None of that matters to me if you're not here. It will be too quiet. What am I supposed to do? Talk to Mom? No, thanks. You say we can talk and text and it will be just like normal, but it won't be for me. [*Pause.*] Believe it or not, even when I am being a jerk, I like having you as my older sister. I know I'm supposed to be too cool to admit it, but I'm not. I'm telling you the truth for once. Without you here, I'm just me. And that's not enough.

MATZOH

Carol L. Lashof

Comic
AVI, 8

AVI *is talking to his or her best friend at lunchtime in the elementary school cafeteria. The two children always share their lunches, but today is different.*

AVI   I'm not being mean. I can't share my peanut butter and jelly with you today because today I don't have peanut butter and jelly. Today I have matzoh. And also a hard-boiled egg and this apple stuff. You wanna try it? I'm not gonna have bread for eight whole days because it's Passover. We don't eat bread when it's Passover. So I can't trade. No cookies either, cuz they're against the rules too. Even Oreos. But it's okay for you to eat matzoh. Everybody can eat matzoh. Why don't you want to try it? You're allowed to eat bread and cookies because you're not Jewish, you're Christmas. It's forever until Christmas. But Passover is now. Passover is when all your cousins and aunts and uncles and everybody comes over for dinner, and you get to lie around on pillows and stay up past your bedtime, and you sing a whole bunch of songs, and everybody gets really loud, even the grown-ups, and you tell the story about the Jewish people running away from slavery in Egypt. And, see, the thing is, when you're running away to freedom, you don't have time to wait for the bread to rise, you have to cook it flat. That's matzoh. And we eat it now, even though the whole story happened a way long time ago, because when you eat matzoh, it's special.

Because it helps you remember the story. Also it's yummy.

You wanna try it? It's extra good if you put a glob of the apple stuff on top. [*Pause.*] See, I told you it was good.

MAXINE

Gerry Sheridan

Seriocomic
MAXINE, 13

MAXINE *is talking to her best friend, Midge. They are at home in Maxine's bedroom and her show is opening the next day. She is excited about it.*

MAXINE   I'm so excited—I'm appearing in this play at a place called Where Eagles Dare. It's kind of a black box, but it's one of the really nice black boxes, you know? My mother said I could do it because it's summer. Anyway, I was so happy when I got it, because I had been to like a hundred and fifty auditions and I didn't get anything. I kept doing this monologue and I couldn't get it right. I even taped myself and I thought I sounded horrible. So the show is a really good thing—only problem is I'm getting a crush on the kid playing opposite me. Which is such a stupid cliché and everything. It all started when I felt rehearsals were going badly, so I figured I'd better flirt with him to help things along. I knew I shouldn't be doing it, but I thought it was good for the play. But in the process of making him like me, I start liking him. My mother would kill me if she knew. She thinks this is an enriching activity. I want this to go away. I even opened my Bible for inspiration one day, but unfortunately I read, "Love thy neighbor as yourself," which I then interpreted for my own purposes. I've been so upset about it that I lost my cell phone and sprained my ankle. I was really happy one day in rehearsal when he argued for like ten minutes with the director over the difference between an action and an objective. He yelled, "I bet you don't even know what an objective is!" It went on and on and I was really happy because he was acting like a total tool and I hated him at that moment, but it only lasted twenty-four hours. By next rehearsal I had a crush on him again. But anyway, it's really good that I'm doing this show because of my cousin, who makes fun of me for taking acting and singing lessons. So now I can show him, 'cause I'm telling my whole family I'm on Broadway.

MY ROOM
Charles Belov

Dramatic
BEN, 14 to 15

BEN *has been referred to juvenile court for psychiatric evaluation after having essentially destroyed the contents of his bedroom. He is speaking to a therapist.*

BEN   Order frightens me. The thought of coming home from school, walking into my room, and having a place for everything and everything in its place fills me with terror. My video games in the bookcase, the controls in the drawer under the TV, the bed made, no leftover pizza from three days ago, petrifying. So a year ago I put a lock on the door, so my mom can't get in and clean. Anyway, I get home from school yesterday, and the lock is gone and it's been replaced with a regular doorknob. Everything in that room is at right angles to everything else. Not a spot of food anywhere. I storm into the kitchen and my mom's there and I yell at her, "What did you do to my room?" And she's all, "We had to clean it, dear, it was drawing ants." And I start cursing and screaming and my dad comes in with his belt off—did I tell you he believes in spanking?—and he's like, "You shut up right now and go to your room, or you're going to get it." Oh, and he drinks, too. So I head back to my room and I shut the door and push the bed up against it so they can't open it. And I start throwing everything off my bookshelves onto the floor. Then I pick up a book and rip a page out. Then I rip another page out. A third page. Fourth. Fifth. When I get to the end of the book I pick up another one. One page. Two. Three. And another book. I'm getting paper cuts here and there and I don't care. Did I mention they're knocking on the door every fifteen or ten or five or two minutes? "I'm studying!" I yell. "Open the door. We want to see you," my mom says. And Dad's all like, "You apologize to your mother." And Mom is all, "We just want what's best for you." Meanwhile, I've started on my pile of CDs that I haven't touched in five years because it's all in the cloud and I break one. Then another. Then another. They all come apart with this satisfying snap. Video games out of their packages. Bedsheets onto the floor. Three hours. An incredibly satisfying mess everywhere. And finally, there's nothing more to destroy. And wouldn't you know, they've called the police! "Come out here, son. We just want to talk to you." That's the cop, not my parents. I'm not their son. "I'm just studying!" And I look out the window and I see my father has put a ladder up against the side of the house and he's staring into my bedroom with this look of horror in his eyes and his face all curled up in rage. And I know that my tired arms and hands and paper cuts are a badge of honor, that I have done the right thing. And even if you put me away, I won't have to deal with my mother cleaning my room ever again.

OVERNIGHT
Libby Emmons

Dramatic
LILY, 13

LILY *lives in the New Jersey woods with her brother and her mom. She gets teased a lot at school, and her mom is pretty unavailable. Her brother is mean, and she likes the time alone, just as the sun's coming up, with everyone in the house asleep. She lies back on the grass and looks at the sky.*

LILY   Layin' there on my back like I always do. Sorta cold, but y'know, I'm always kinda' cold—and the grass under me is sorta soft—an' I sorta melt in, a little niche just for me an' my ass. I'd lay my palms out flat, an' lift 'em up again to rub my eyes, always forgetting the little bits of rock stuck to my fingers. But they wouldn't cut me up, just mean there's more to rub away. An' I'm watchin' the sky 'cause I always do, and the stars are all bustin' themselves up with sparkles like dust, fairy dust or somethin'. And so I'm rippin' at the grass, pullin' up the dirt. The air all around was so dark, like mud I thought, and the grains of it were all around me— purple and red—almost made it hard to see the sky. Funny, the air gettin' in the way of the sky. An' I reached down to scratch my toe an' caught this bug in my hand, the bug that was tickling at my foot. A bloodsucker, a little tic— dug into the palm of my hand an' I watched it grow fatter and fatter. Jus' suckin' on my blood—the way the air does, an' the grass does. An' I started wonderin' why everything seems to be suckin' on me, or expectin' me to give. Almost no control over the bloodsucker bug—over what it does or what it takes. But choice, I guess, an' that's the same dif- ference, right? So I pulled the safety pin outa' my sleeve an' poked at it, denting the skin a little all over, until it ripped and popped—same way as mine does if I poke at it for long enough an' hard enough—an' the blood spread all through my fingers. An' I went to wipe it on the grass, the bug's little legs still stuck into me, 'til I realized it was my own blood. I licked it off, sucked it off my fingers, 'cause it was my blood, an' I wanted to have it back for my own. I wanted my whole self to be that red color—same as my blood and the specs in the air—an' I wanted to jump into the sky. A big red star. But I knew I couldn't. So I lay back down again an' the grass ain't so soft as clouds, jus' feels like it's pullin' me in, an' I realize the sky's the only place to be, the only place to stay clear and glitter like crazy.

PANDA TV
Mark Andrew

Seriocomic
CHELSEA, 14

CHELSEA *has started a campaign to support panda breeding in zoos, which has sparked national interest. She is being interviewed on TV, and the reporter gets an unexpectedly full and rich answer to the question: "What made you think of pandas,* CHELSEA*?"*

CHELSEA The first thing I figured out, I mean the *very* first thing I can remember making a proper decision about, was, How long is this worth thinking about? I was about six when I figured it out, and the TV news kept ending every night with the weather report, like it still does, every night, right after tea. Dad would watch the sports report, and I'd watch Dad watching the sports results—which is funny because he gets so serious—then Mum would come in from the garden, and we'd all watch the weather forecast. And every night there was this big whoo-haah, I know that's not a real word, about barometric pressure (I looked *that* right up) and air movement and rain and sun and wind, and I mean, really, here, in New York? I figured there were five main weather patterns, and so I said to Mum and Dad, why don't they just say tomorrow is a number three day? It would save time, and be more accurate, and that way it would leave time for more important news, like that panda at the zoo that won't make a baby, because if people would listen to that more, we'd figure out a way to help her and there'd be more pandas and you can't tell me that's not more important than if you get caught without an umbrella. I wondered what that panda was thinking. I thought about that a lot. I imagined the baby panda, not even started inside, saying it wasn't ready, and the big panda just somehow held it inside, all safe, like an idea waiting to be thought, and she told it there was no rush. I figured the big panda might say, You wait until you're good and ready, because it's not as if there's any panda-TV now, is there? That made me laugh, and Dad looked up from his newspaper and asked what was so funny, and I said it was a panda joke he wouldn't understand, and he seemed pretty happy about that. We need more time for the important stuff, the real news. I mean some of it's different each day, apart from Iraq and climate change and the stock market. They should use that number system for the economy too, so that the newsreader would say today was a type four day. And if the weather and the stock market were the same number we'd all say, of course! The rain came, the crops are okay so the farmers can feed the miners and the train drivers get a feed too, maybe a nice salad wholemeal roll if they think about their guts, sitting down for hours, while they're hauling the train from the mine to the coast and then the ships will keep sailing to Japan, and wherever else the iron ore goes to make the cars so we can relax so we can go to work and pay for all the stuff. It's not as complicated as the TV makes out, but then that's its job I guess, or we wouldn't need so many lawyers and politicians. Maybe the news should be more about the panda, and it would only get interrupted if the numbers were very different, which mostly they aren't.

PARKER

Deanna Alisa Ableser

Comic
PARKER, 12 to 14

PARKER *is slightly awkward looking but definitely on the cuter side. He is getting ready to ask a girl out. He is speaking to the audience.*

PARKER   It's only a school dance . . . a seriously lame middle school dance. I mean, how hard could it possibly be? I can walk. I can talk. I can manage going up to a girl and asking her to dance. I can do it. I can totally do it. Just take a deep breath, man . . . a really really deep breath. Put one foot in front of the other and move forward. Good! Great! Phe-nomenal! I'm walking . . . walking towards her . . . walking towards the most beautiful girl in the entire school and I *am going* to ask her to the dance. *The fall dance. This Friday. After school. In less than twenty-four hours.*

[*Starts hyperventilating and stops walking, hitting himself in the head.*]

Seriously, what could I possibly be thinking? I can't just go up to her and ask her out. She'll laugh right in my face. Then she'll laugh with her friends. Then her friends will start laughing and their friends will start laughing and pretty soon, and don't think I'm overexaggerating here, the entire middle school will be laughing . . . and laughing at me. Next thing you know, I'll be on the morning announcements and they'll announce that I'm officially the biggest loser of the entire school. That's it. There's no way I'm asking her. No way. Phew! I feel so much better . . . I mean, to think that I was actually going to . . .

[*Starts walking forward.*]

Hey, what's going on? Where ya going, feet? You're going in the wrong direction! You're walking towards her! Stop! Stop! Stop, I tell you, for the love of all that is good in this world, stop!

[*He stops.*]

Thank you. *Thank* you! Thank *you*! I thought you were going to be stupid enough to walk up to the most beautiful girl in the entire school and ask her to the dance. Let me tell you feet, *that* would just have been stupid. Plain stupid. I mean, stupid to the . . .

[*Still looking at his feet.*]

Excuse me?

[*Slowly looking up and talking to girl's feet.*]

You'll what?

[*Continuing to look up and looking at girl's face.*]

You're serious?!

[*With a broad smile.*]

With me?! You'll go to the dance with *me*!

[*Jumps up in excitement and looks back down at feet.*]

I have the best feet in the entire world.

THE PEANUT ALLERGY
Kayla Cagan

Dramatic
CRICKET, 7

CRICKET *explains why her little brother, Henry, aged 5, can't eat peanuts.*

CRICKET Ever since Henry was born, he's been special. Everybody in the whole family knew it. They said I was special because I was the first girl born and he was special because he was the first boy born and I was extraspecial because I was also the first big sister. Mama said it was my job to help Henry understand the world, which is pretty funny because the world is pretty big and I don't know if I understand the whole thing. Like I don't understand why some dogs and cats don't like each other. I like both of them. They are both cute and cuddly and cats are funny because they poop in a box. Dogs are always giving kisses. They should just like each other. And there's another thing I don't understand. I can eat all of the peanut butter and jelly sandwiches I want. I can eat them for breakfast, lunch, and dinner. But Mama and Daddy said there's no way Henry can have peanut butter, not ever. Not even once. And he can't have peanuts, either, because Mama says he has a peanut allergy. I don't know why I can eat peanuts and he can't. I don't exactly know what an allergy is, but I do know that Henry had peanuts once when he was just three years old and he got really sick. He got so sick he had to go to the hospital and Mama couldn't stop crying, which made me cry, too. Daddy told me that Henry would be okay, but somehow I felt like it was all my fault. Wasn't I supposed to help him understand the world? Wasn't I supposed to protect him from dangerous things? How could I have let it happen? I didn't know that peanuts would hurt him and Mama and Daddy said it wasn't my fault, but I felt really bad. Now when I look at Henry, all I want to do is protect him. I can't let anything—or anyone—ever hurt my little brother again. I'm his big sister, after all.

PENDRAGON COUNTY GHOSTS
Don Nigro

Dramatic
DOLLY, 12

In 1941, in a small town in eastern Ohio, DOLLY CASEY, age 12, a very smart and determined girl, has escaped from the children's services people and come to find her Uncle Jimmy, her mother's brother, in an attempt to convince him to take her and her sister Winny in to live with him. Their mother has abandoned them, the authorities have decided that Winny is mentally ill, and they have put her in a mental health facility. But DOLLY has run away to find Jimmy and persuade him to give them a home. She is desperate. This is the most important thing in her life.

DOLLY   You got to listen to me, Uncle Jimmy. I know you don't know Winny and me all that well since we were little, because Mama was always dragging us off to East Liverpool and Pittsburgh and Wellsville and all kinds of places, but you're the only person I could come to. You got to help me get Winny out of that place. She's not crazy, but she'll go crazy in a place like that. I know she will. Uncle Jimmy, I never asked you for anything before in my whole life, and I'll never ask you for anything again, I swear, but you got to do this one thing for me. Mama's gone, and Winny doesn't belong in a place for crazy people. She's just a little girl, and she's not crazy, she's just different, and I told them I'd take care of her, but they said I can't, that I'm too young. But that's stupid, because I been taking care of her for just about her whole life. It's not Mama's fault. Mama just carries around so much unhappiness in her heart there isn't much room left for us. But she loves us. I know she loves us. But she can't take care of us. Uncle Jimmy, I know you keep to yourself, mostly, fixing up old cars and fixing up those old pianos Great Uncle Willy piled up in the barn. I know you can fix pretty much anything. Well, you got to fix this. You got to come down to that place with me and get my little sister out of there, and you got let us come live with you. I won't make any trouble, I swear. I can cook. I'll clean the house. I'll take care of Winny. You won't even know we're here. Please. You got to do this. You got to. She's just gonna wither up and die in that place. I know you're a good person. I used to bring Winny over here sometimes and sit out behind the barn in the evening and listen to you play those old pianos, and Winny would hear that music and she'd calm right down. I think she could be happy here. I know it's a lot to ask. I know you're used to being alone, but Uncle Jimmy, I think maybe there's a time in a person's life when they get a chance to maybe not be alone, and I figure this is your chance. And our chance. And I got no place else to go. So don't you go telling me you're sorry. I don't want to hear that. You just get in that Chevy and drive me down there, right now, because I'm not letting my sister stay in that place one more night, do you hear me? Not one more night.

PENDRAGON COUNTY GHOSTS
Don Nigro

Dramatic
WINNY, 11

In 1941, in a mental institution in eastern Ohio, WINNY CASEY, age 11, is telling us about her mother's dreams of wolves. WINNY's mother has abandoned her and her sister, Dolly, and WINNY has been put here because the authorities think she's mentally ill, but mostly WINNY is just different, and in despair. She misses her mother very much, and now Dolly has run off to get help, and WINNY, feeling completely abandoned, remembers how safe she used to feel in the arms of her highly unstable and troubled mother.

WINNY   Just at midnight I heard a noise out my window, in the woods. A dead branch falling from a tree, maybe. Or maybe something else is out there. Mama used to dream about wolves. My mother is very beautiful, although I know she's crazy. Her eyes are just like mine. She took us away when we were little girls. She said it was to save us from the wolves. I remember her standing at the window, looking at the moon. When the moon is full, she said, your father turns into a wolf. She loves to sit in the dark with us. We cuddle together under a blanket because we didn't pay the heating bill, drinking cola and eating potato chips, and listening to *The Shadow* on the radio. We feel very safe together, my sister and me, under the blanket with my mother. Safe from wolves. It was those times I loved her the most. Her face was so beautiful in the blinking light from the dance hall across the street. The wolves will never find us here, I thought. But I know they are still out there in the dark. I like being surrounded by walls, blankets, my mother's arms. She smells like shampoo and flowers and chocolate, and cigarettes and whisky. I was always scared that one day the wolves would get in the house and take her away from us, and put her in a place full of mad people. A place like this. That's why we moved so often. But in the end, the wolves always find you. I can see their red eyes glowing out the window in the dark.

PENDRAGON COUNTY GHOSTS
Don Nigro

Dramatic
WINNY, 11

In 1941, in a small town in eastern Ohio, WINNY CASEY, *age 11, has been put in a mental institution after her mother has abandoned her and her sister, Dolly. Dolly has escaped to try and get help from their Uncle Jimmy, their mother's brother, who is their last chance to stay together and have a home. But* WINNY *is alone now in the mental institution, in despair and feeling utterly abandoned. She is talking to us about the nature of ghosts, which she feels are everywhere.*

WINNY   This is a place which is famous for its ghosts but only among the people who live here because this is mostly a forgotten place, and there's a lot to be said for forgotten places and lost places, and Pendragon County is a lost and mostly forgotten place in the eastern part of Ohio, which is full of ghosts of all sorts, which is why I like it so much here. There's Indian ghosts in the caves on the old Pendragon property and the Ghost Hill across from the Burgundy Inn, and the Red Rose Inn is full of ghosts and my dead Grandma Flowers's boarding hotel, which has ghostly persons moving up and down the corridors at all hours, which I know because my mother and my sister Dolly and I have lived there on several occasions when we were passing through on the way to some other place. I think sometimes the ghosts get into people's heads and then they can't get out, and that's why people are so unhappy, like Mama. It isn't that unhappy people don't love anybody. Sometimes it's that they love people so much they go crazy. Love scares you and makes you crazy. It's what I learned

110

from Mama. And love is full of ghosts. And the ghosts are everywhere. You can't get away from them. When I used to sit outside Great Uncle Willy's old barn with my sister Dolly and listen to my Uncle Jimmy play the piano, I could hear the ghosts in the music. I can't always hear them in music, but when my Uncle Jimmy played, I could hear them. My Uncle Jimmy's music was always full of ghosts.

PLAYER 10
Joël Doty

Comic
MIKE, 12 to 14

MIKE *has reported for Little League practice. He's talking to his coach.*

MIKE Right here, Coach. I'm Mike. Oh. Mike B. Not Mike D. Sure. I'm Player 10. Watch your shoes, Mike. Boy, did that other team just get lucky. Last week I took out a catcher. Messed his knee up real good. I saw that fastball comin' and POW! I would have hit it over the fence except my shoes kind of slipped in the dirt. I asked the coach if he thought the team should sue the field maintenance people, but he said it wouldn't be good publicity and besides it was the catcher who got hurt when I fell. Don't forget bug spray, Mike. Who wants to stand in a bunch of weeds and get hot and sweaty, anyway? I already got two, three, four, five mosquito bites, and I know there's a bees nest out there somewhere on top of the fence. It's not that I'm scared of bees or mosquitoes. I'm not scared of anything. Except being allergic. I fell into a hive last year and swelled up like a blowfish I saw in the aquarium. Do you know how big a blowfish gets? At least I got ice cream in the hospital. The team is supposed to go for ice cream when we win. But when your hat falls off and the sun is in your eyes and there's a bunch of bugs out to sting you, it's hard to see a ball in the air or find it behind you in a hole. I bet even Mike B. couldn't do that. We went home in our own cars instead of jumping in the coach's van to get Dairy Queen. I like being Player 10. Player 10 doesn't have to deal with weeds or stings or itching or sunstroke or heart failure or broken bones or dropping a ball and getting the frozen treatment. Player 10 has it made. I wouldn't trade to be Player 9 or 8 or 7 or— . . . Wha'd you say coach? Right field? Spray me down!

THE POWER OF BIRDS
Robin Rice Lichtig

Dramatic
ZOE, 10 to 12

ZOE *is in Sunday school. The lesson bores her. She looks at paintings that hang on the walls and daydreams. She thinks her father might be Jesus.*

ZOE   Jesus sits under a tree with a bunch of little kids around him. He tells them a story. The sun shines. The little kids are mostly blonde. Their clothes are clean and ironed. I don't know why they're sitting around when it's a beautiful day. There's a hill with grass and flowers. There's birds in a nest and a river down the hill, but they're sitting there looking at Jesus and listening to the story. It's an amazing story. Or else they're just posing for the picture. The other painting's better. Jesus standing in a forest. A sparrow is on his shoulder. All kinds of other birds are eating seeds at his feet. A squirrel, a chipmunk, and a mouse are eating seeds, too. A copper beetle is climbing a tree trunk. A leopard is peeking out of the bushes. Three spider monkeys are in the trees. Some kind of deer with horns is over in a corner. It has a good feeling. Get inside it. Get right in the tree with the monkeys. Or curl up by the deer. Lay on the moss. Breathe: in with the tree roots, out with the leaves, in with the wind, out with the sun. Open your ears like shells.

[Makes sounds of the forest.]

Russstle-russsstle-russtle, whoooosshh, peep-peep, peep-peep, tick-tick-tick, swiiiissshh . . . The deer shifts to get more comfortable. Put a hand on her side. Feel her breathing. Breathe like grass. An ant backs over my ankle, pulling an oak leaf. The copper beetle pinches down the tree and clumps into the woods. A finch eyes the beetle, but lets it go. The leopard traps her tail under a paw and licks the tip. A crow hops over, up on my leg. She's got her eye on my silver barrette. Daddy will tell her to wait while I take it off. She flies away and puts it in her nest. Somewhere in the world there is a piece of me in a nest in a tree in a forest for always.

PUBLIC SPEAKING AND THE ADVENTURES OF HUCKLEBERRY FINN

Martha Patterson

Seriocomic
TOMMY, 13 to 15

TOMMY is delivering a speech to his class on the subject of censorship. He wears glasses and looks very studious and serious. He is standing in front of his teacher's desk holding his notes. There is a glass of water on the desk.

TOMMY *The Adventures of Huckleberry Finn*. The *original* version. Not the new one.

[*He ruffles through his notes, then puts them aside.*]

I really think I'd rather speak spontaneously. Mr. Simpson wanted us to feel free in this exercise to follow our train of thought, even though he also wanted us to be prepared. I think, for a class in public speaking, it's good to be spontaneous.

[*He drinks from the glass of water.*]

In the old version of *Huck Finn*, Mark Twain used the word "nigger" when Huck describes his friend, Jim. But in the new version they took that word out. They changed it to "slave." The very thing Jim ran away to escape. The thing is, Mark Twain didn't call Jim a "slave." He didn't have Huck use that word at all. Huck called Jim a "nigger," a word that was in common use at the time. Doesn't it seem wrong to change a classic, to alter the words of a man who really must have known what he was doing with words? And to rewrite the way people actually spoke at the time? I laughed out loud when I read *Huckleberry Finn*. It's a great story about a deep friendship between two unlikely friends.

[*He pauses, and adjusts his glasses.*]

But I digress. If you wrote a story about your first crush, would you want someone a hundred years later to "clean it up?" To make it acceptable to the ears of people living in the twenty-second century? Because probably people won't talk the same way then. We might sound very inappropriate to them. Think about it. "I made out with her and it was cosmic, man!" "When he touched her he felt fire burning in his loins!" "She had a rack like Scarlett Johansson." Are those expressions acceptable today for a kid my age? Will they be a hundred years from now? Today we use the word "black" for African Americans. But that wasn't even acceptable at one time, then it became acceptable again, and it may not be acceptable in a hundred years. Do you really want some bogus editor in the future to clean up your language? [*Beat.*] I don't want great literature cleaned up. I don't *accept* it cleaned up. And I like *Huckleberry Finn* just the way it always was.

[*He picks up his sheaf of papers and bows.*]

Thank you.

RUDY
Elayne Heilveil

Dramatic
RUBY, 9 to 11

RUBY, *a farm girl, is talking to her father.*

RUBY   Oh Papa, the carnival is comin' to town! Can we go? I
wanna go for a ride. Round and round on the carousel.

[*She spins around, looking up at the sky.*]

Remember? I looked up at the lights and said they looked
like a circle of stars. "How far are the stars, Papa?" And you
said, they're as far as forever. [*Beat.*] I miss Mama. She told
me my life would be bigger than this front porch. You're
gonna own the world, she said. Oh Papa, let's find Rudy.
You know, the horse on the carousel. I was so scared when
I was small. They looked so big. And you lifted me up and
took my hand and walked me past every one. "How 'bout
this one," you said. "Oh no, not that one, Papa, he looks too
mean." "Or that one, the one with a jewel in the middle of
his forehead," you asked.

"That's the one I want, the one with the jewel." And you told
me it was a ruby. Just like me. And that I was a special gem
named after the month that I was born. You told me to rub
the magic jewel between his eyes and make a wish. "Rub
the Rudy?" I said. You laughed. "Rudy? Well then, we'll call
him Rudy." And you lifted me up on his back and we spun
round and round and I looked up at the sky. They looked
like puffs of clouds. You said they were angels lookin' down
and I'd never need to be scared again. I closed my eyes and
heard the music, up and down and round and round and

I thought it was the angels singin' their song just for me. Sometimes, when I'm scared, I hear that song in my head. And I think Mama's up there, singin' with the angels. Lookin' down. [*Beat.*] Let's find Rudy, Papa. I wanna make a wish.

SAFE
Penny Jackson

Dramatic
NINA, 14

NINA *is talking to her middle school psychologist at her Upper East Side, New York, private girls' school.*

NINA   Food doesn't make me happy. But that doesn't mean I can't stop eating. My dad says I should exercise more. What he's really saying is why don't I look like his twenty-five-year-old Russian model girlfriend? You know my mom's an alkie. Sorry, alcoholic. But I don't think vodka makes my mom happy. But vodka's not food, is it? Do I think I'm fat? I think if I lived in Omaha, Nebraska, I would be just fine. Healthy is what they would call me. A big but normal girl. Did you know I found a tub of lard in my locker? Like what is lard? How did those girls find it and why? I also found several boxes of frozen Weight Watchers meals. And yes, they melted all over my books. My school locker's not a friggin' refrigerator. Those anorexic senior bitches were really pushing me. But screw them. No one can bully me into puking after every meal. Sorry, Dr. Schwartz. Just a little stressed about midterms. When was the last time I was happy? Let me think . . . When I was nine. I was happy during my ninth-birthday party. My mom wasn't drinking then. My dad was still there. All my friends were nice to me and we jumped up and down on the trampoline. And I felt so wonderful. I was jumping so high that I could almost touch the ceiling. Nothing was holding me back. I was floating in the air. Like a feather. And I'd do anything . . . just anything . . . to feel that free again.

SECOND THOUGHTS
Melanie Bean

Seriocomic
ANNA, 10

In this direct address to the audience, ANNA *reflects on her decision not to try on her mother's bra.*

ANNA   I picked up my mother's bra this morning. I was going to try it on, but then I got that sneaky feeling and stopped. She wouldn't mind. I'm pretty sure about that. In my mind I could see the dial and the needle. That's what made me stop. The needle went up from the green part to the yellow, so I stopped. The dial is in my head, and Mom says that's a very good thing. She calls it "our moral compass." The yellow means "maybe." I think I'd rather have a real compass. And I'd take it with me on a trip. I would be out on a road and follow it till I had to make a turn. Then I'd check the compass and go left. Or go right. I'd follow the arrow and keep going. I might go farther than I've ever been, out in the country with the fences and the barns and the cows. Maybe I'd have my bike. That would be faster. I could strap the compass onto the handlebars. I could carry a map in my backpack just in case there's no cell service. But the compass would help me get home, too. [*Pause.*] I really like cows. I like the way they know what they're doing. Maybe a thunderstorm would upset them, but usually they're so . . . comfortable. And they're friendly, if they feel like it. One will walk over and look you in the eye and give you a message. And then another one comes over and says hello. And it would be okay even if there was no fence. I could spend the afternoon with them. I wish school was like that. I even wish there were fences in school so you could tell who's friendly—for real. Mom says I'll figure it out.

SEVEN CHANNELS
David L. Epstein

Dramatic
KATHY, 15

KATHY is a smart student who spent a summer away from home in a prestigious urban art program. When she returns to her midwestern home, she takes up issues with her parents who are barely prepared for her assault.

KATHY   What's my problem?! You picked me up from the bus stop exactly one hour ago, we sat at dinner for ten minutes, and in that time you've managed to insult every creed, religion, and race that crosses your mind. First of all, American Indians are not "greedy" because they run casinos. They were gifted those plots of land and licenses to make up for the decimation of their people! African Americans are not the "most racist people you know," because you don't *know* any African Americans! I mean, have you ever actually talked to a black person, Dad?! And there is nothing wrong with Mexicans or Hispanics or anyone from Central America. They aren't "dirty people" getting in the way of your construction business. And the Chinese aren't taking over the world—they just, and I know this is hard to believe, happen to be doing *way better than us!* Yes, there are problems. But where is your heart? Where is your compassion? Immigrants come to the United States because it's the last chance for any semblance of a good, decent life. Don't you ever stop to ask yourself, what if that was me? What if things were so bad that the only way you could protect your daughter was to send me to another country, alone, with a hundred other refugee children? Under those circumstances, you'd be on your knees praying for the compassion of strangers more fortunate than you! It is so upsetting to learn that everything you taught me is wrong, that your value system is so low, that you have such little regard for anyone beyond the border of your own small world! I love you and always will. But I cannot tell you how disappointed I am in you. You know those old televisions? The big boxy ones with a dial to turn the channel? That's you. Seven channels and all of them as white as snow.

STRANGE ATTRACTIONS
David L. Epstein

Dramatic
LINA, 13 to 15

LINA *is rebellious and beginning to see that the world is larger than her suburban roots. She is affected emotionally when she realizes that not all governments treat their citizens the same. Here, she addresses the audience directly.*

LINA   Did you know there are no old-age homes in Malaysia? You probably don't even know where Malaysia is. It has is a thriving economy so it's not that they can't afford housing for old people—they just don't have it. And the reason is because Malaysian families stay together. It's part of the culture. The old and the young. Cousins. Uncles. Everybody takes care of each other. Baby crying in one room, elderly dying in the next. If we lived there, we'd pool our money and *vote* on what to do with it. If one of us got married, both families would move right in together. Sometimes there can be twenty people living under one roof—but it works! Malaysia has the lowest crime rate in the world next to like Amsterdam or something because the old and the young are kept together, which makes them able to communicate and understand each other and learn! To want to leave the family and make a life on your own makes no sense to a Malaysian. To them, nothing is better than gathering at the table with everyone you love and sharing a meal. To them, Thanksgiving is every night!

[*Defeated.*]

Why are we so backward from this? Why are we so different? Parents want to get rid of kids the moment they turn eighteen. Kids want to get rid of parents. Old people are stored away in closets when they are no longer useful. That scares me. We're fine now. We're young. But what about later? I don't want to end up in an old-age home. Should I leave here? Should I move to Malaysia?

SWEET TEMPERED
Barry Eitel

Comic
SARAH, 10 to 12

SARAH *is at a malt shop in the 1920s. She's waiting for her mother*
to pick her up and is chatting away at the server.

SARAH   I really like horses. My mother has a book with a lot
of paintings of horses. White ones, black ones, brown ones,
spotted ones. My favorite is the spotted ones. They look like
a blanket, I think. Sometimes I wish I was a horse. Except
I don't think horses can eat candy bars. And that would
make me real blue. My favorite candy bar is Baby Ruth. My
mother says candy is really good for me because it keeps
me sweet tempered. She says I should have a little every
day. She's a really sweet lady. And she's really smart! But
she's afraid of the dark, and I love the dark. It's the only time
there is any adventure. I don't go in for that girl stuff—dolls
or hopscotch or any of that rubbish. I really like baseball. I
like anything where you get to hit something really hard,
actually. I'm trying to learn navigation, because I'm train-
ing to be a pilot when I grow up. Girls are pilots now, too,
even though the fellas at school laugh at me when I tell
them about it. I'll be the one laughing when I'm soaring
hundreds of miles above the ground. I'll wave to them from
my shiny little airplane, with my goggles and leather jacket.
Maybe I'll even drop something on them. A Baby Ruth, so
they know it's me! That's it!

TARA'S LAMENT
Mark Lambeck

Comic
TARA, 15

TARA, *an overweight 15-year-old, has been on a diet and she can't take it anymore, as she rants to her sister.*

TARA   I can't stand it anymore! I've been on this diet for three days . . .

[*Looks at her watch.*]

   . . . six hours and twenty-two minutes and I've had it. That's it.

[*She starts pacing around the room.*]

   I can't take it anymore. I admit it . . . I've failed. I'm weak. Okay? I surrender. You win. You're the stronger sister! Read my lips—I am not drinking any more powdered protein shakes. I'm chucking Mom's blender and going back to real food. I mean real, solid, tantalize-your-taste buds, greasy American eats. I'm talking hard-core, tongue-teasing FOOD! I'm talking pizza with extra cheese, pepperoni, onions, olives, and mushrooms. I'm talking brownies. I'm talking chocolate chip cookies. I want a bag of Wise extra crispy, sour cream and onion family-size potato chips. I want ice cream NOT frozen yogurt. [*Catches her breath.*] *And I don't mean vanilla. I want DOUBLE-DUTCH CHOCOLATE ALMOND SUPREME. I want it with hot fudge sauce and crushed nuts. I want seven-layer chocolate mousse cake with whipped cream and a glass of iced tea with three—count them, THREE—sugars. And I want it NOW!*

[*Pause. Takes a deep breath.*]

Oh God, I'm shaking.

[*Juts her hands out in front of her to show them.*]

Do you see that? I'm actually shaking. Oh my God. I'm okay.
All right. I know Kaitlyn is going to be disappointed, but I
don't care. I'm not taking kickboxing class with her anymore. My legs hurt. My arms hurt. My butt is sore.

[*Sarcastically:*]

And I'm just a tiny bit cranky.

[*Pause. Feels her forehead.*] I feel light-headed. This lack of
food has deprived my brain of oxygen. Okay, okay. Deep
breaths. [*She takes a few deep breaths.*] I just need a few
deep breaths. All right. Okay. I'm all right. I need to get a
grip. Just a few seconds to get a grip . . . a grip [*EXPLODES.*]
. . . around a taco or a cheeseburger or a Twinkie! [*Pause.
Quizzically.*] Do they still make those?

[*Composing herself.*] Okay. All right. I'm awright.

[*Lamenting.*] Look. You're my sister and I really do appreci-
ate that you're looking out for me. I know you got rid of all
the junk food in this house. You said it's for my own good. I
get it. I know I don't have a prayer of finding anything with
the words "Fritos" or "Little Debbie" on it. But I also know
this is not a momentary lapse. This will not pass like . . .
Dad's kidney stone. This requires chocolate intervention!

You are looking at a desperate girl here. I'm standing here
in jeans whose zipper is holding on by the edges of its
teeth and I need sweet gratification!!!

So listen up! I'm only gonna say this once. If I don't get

something smothered in chocolate into my mouth within the next few minutes, I can no longer be held responsible for my actions.

[*Blackout.*]

TOURISTS OF THE MINEFIELD

Glenn Alterman

Dramatic
ELIZABETH, 14

ELIZABETH *may have met the "right" guy at a party.*

ELIZABETH   I just needed to get away from all that noise, you know? It's so crowded in there. I like to come out here by the lake sometimes, look up at the stars. So calm, quiet. [*Pause.*] Y'know, sometimes, sometimes I feel like I'm from another planet, isn't that crazy? Like I just somehow ended up here on earth. That I'm actually a whole different species. And I don't understand the people here. I mean, I look at them in there, watch their mouths move, hear their words, but I really have no idea what any of them are saying. Have no idea what they mean; isn't that weird? . . . I saw you standing there in the corner, and there was just, I don't know, something in your *eyes*. Way you were just staring up at the ceiling. And the way you were leaning on that wall, like you were trying to hold it up or something. And when I came over, said hello, the way you stared at me like you knew me, or wanted too. . . . I kinda feel like we do know each other, sort of, in some way. Isn't that crazy? . . . Hey, you don't have to say anything. We can just sit here, quiet, look up at the sky. . . . I like when it's quiet like this. [*Beat. Looking up.*] It's a really nice night, isn't it?

TOURISTS OF THE MINEFIELD
Glenn Alterman

Dramatic
STEPHANIE, 14 to 15

This is an inner monologue in which STEPHANIE *thinks about her hatred for a "supposed" friend.*

STEPHANIE   You are so transparent. Everything you think you're hiding is so *obvious.* Do you think I can't see your hate? Hel-lo! It's right there on your face—in Technicolor! And that's fine with me. Because I hate you, too. I do. And like you, I've been trying to hide my hate. But it's just a waste of time, and energy. We pass each other in the hall at school, say hello. But blood is dripping from your over-made-up eyes. We both say (too sweetly) "Hi, how are you?" when we secretly despise each other. Waste of time. Waste of energy. I mean wouldn't it be nice if we could stop in the hall and smile. And say, "I hate you!" And yell, "And you hate me, too!" Then just keep walking to our next class. [*Beat.*] I hate your hellos. Next time I see you, I think I'll tell you so. Actually, I hate everything about you. Now stick that in your backpack! [*Beat. Too sweet.*] Oh, yeah, "Have a nice day."

A TRIP TO THE PRINCIPAL
Phoebe Farmer

Dramatic
ETHAN, 8

ETHAN *is talking to the principal, to whom he has been sent by his teacher.*

ETHAN   I don't know why Anthony Mazzio isn't here—he's the one who should be here—Mrs. Belasconi should've sent *him* to the principal's office, not me. Anthony said it—it's his fault—he started it. Are you gonna call my mom? She was really mad the last time you called her. [*Pause.*] We were in social studies. Mrs. Belasconi was telling us about the Native American tribes in the Great Plains states, and I was listening to her talk, paying good attention to everything she said, and then Anthony leans over to me, like he always does, 'cause he's really annoying like that, and says something . . . I'll show you what happened.

[*He starts acting everything out.*]

So, I'm sitting in my seat, listening about the Indians and the wigwams, and Anthony leans over, like this—

[*He shows it.*]

—and says a bad word, and that's when I tap him and tell him to stop—like this—

[*He shows it.*]

I say, "Anthony, c'mon, STOP!" —and then he throws himself on the floor, like this—

[*He shows it.*]

—and starts crying 'cause he hurt his arm—all dramatic. It's a bad word . . . I'm not allowed to say it . . . well . . . it starts with the letter *s*. But I didn't push him over, that's a lie! I tapped him—it wasn't my fault he fell over—it was just a tap—he falls over all the time—on purpose, just to be annoying. Please don't call her—she doesn't like to be interrupted at work—she'll get really, really mad—her face'll get red, and she'll start blinking her eyes—she says her head could explode.

[*He gets increasingly upset.*]

YOU DON'T UNDERSTAND—SHE GETS CRAZY MAD AT ME—IT'S NOT GOOD FOR HER STRESS LEVEL—THAT'S WHAT SHE SAYS—IT'LL BE MY FAULT—IT'S ALWAYS MY FAULT! PLEASE, MR. FRANCONI, DON'T CALL HER! PROMISE ME YOU WON'T CALL HER!

UN-CHATTY CATHY

Gabriel Davis

Seriocomic
CATHY, 13

CATHY *stands in front of Brian, the boy she has a crush on, by his locker in the hallway at school.*

CATHY   Hello, hi . . . hello. I'm a, um, I'm . . . I'm Cathy. I'm . . . not a chatty Cathy. I'm sort of the inverse of that. An un-chatty Cathy. It's the first time I've heard me talk, too. I mean, the first time I've heard me talk to you. To you in particular. Did you even know my name was Cathy? That I sit behind you in homeroom? I've never seen you look back. I've seen your back, but not you looking back. [*Pause.*] Oh God. So I'm taking this public-speaking class, and now here we are, in public, speaking. But I was hoping it'd be more private. In public-speaking class, they say, tell a story, some anecdote that lets your audience know who you are. When I was six, I was a proud Bluebird of the Camp Fire Girls of America! As a Bluebird, I had to sell mint thins door to door. When my older brother heard, he started laughing. He told my mom, "How is she supposed to sell them if she never makes a peep?"

I could feel my eyes getting a little wet, and I think my mother saw because she said, "They're going to find her so adorable, she won't have to make a peep! And you're going to take her." My mother got me dressed in my official Bluebird outfit—a little white button-up short-sleeve shirt, a knee-length blue skirt, knee-high white socks, white Mary Jane shoes, my hair in pigtails, and my Bluebird pin. She wrote out a little introduction on an index card: "Hello, my name is Cathy and I'm a Bluebird. How would you like to purchase some mint thins to benefit the Campfire Girls of America?" And she included all the details they needed to order the cookies. "See, she's armed with cuteness and the right words." She smiled at me, patting my head. "Now fly, my little Bluebird. Nothing can stop you now!" My brother sighed and took me door to door. He'd wait at the end of each walkway, and I'd make the long walk myself to the front door. My legs would shake. When someone opened, usually a mom—I'd find myself unable to speak. But I had my words. I'd hold out the card and each strange mom at the door would read it, smile, and buy my mint thins. I sold every box. I wanted to tell you that story, because . . . sometimes you have the words, but it's too hard to get them to come out of your mouth. See . . . I know you were going to ask me something . . . but then Patsy told you I think you're ugly, because you have acne and the medicine isn't working. That I'd never go to the dance with you. And that I think you smell like old socks. Well, I didn't say that and I'd rather not say the following out loud so I wrote it.

[CATHY *holds up a large index card that has the words "Patsy is a bitch" written on it. She lowers the first card and holds up another, which says "You're cute." She then holds up another, which says "Be My Dance Date."*]

Well . . . what do you say? I have a blank card, and a pen, if that'd be easier for you.

VOLCANO ON MY FACE
Connie Schindewolf

Comic
MADISON, 13 to 15

MADISON *is talking on the phone to her best friend about her morning discovery. She is looking in the mirror through the entire phone conversation—the mirror ought to be on the "fourth wall" between her and the audience.*

MADISON   Abby, you are not going to believe it, but I woke up with the biggest zit on this planet. Yeah, it's come to a head with all that puss stuff . . . No, I will not pop it! Gross! That is out of the question. So, I'm not going to school today, maybe never! I'm gonna tell my mom I'm sick . . . You know why. I have to give that oral report in English class today. Can you see me getting up in front of those kids to talk about Maya Angelou with this train wreck on my face? I wouldn't even get "I Know Why the Caged Bird Sings" out of my mouth before they'd be falling out of their chairs laughing. I would never be able to step foot in Central High ever, ever again . . . No, I'd have to give the report because it's the last day . . . A Band-Aid? Are you kidding? This thing is so big, that wouldn't cover it. I mean, I would need a full-face mask to cover this honker. That's what my mom says she used to call them when she was in high school. Honkers . . . There is no way cover-up would work. I know, because I already tried it. Looks better at first, and then that awful head just bleeds right through . . . so disgusting! OMG! Abby, the fall play tryouts are today after school. Cody's going to be there, and I was going to ask him to practice with me before so maybe he'd get the idea to ask me to Homecoming. This is just too cruel! And it's right between my eyes! You know, there would be an advantage to having a uni-brow! So, I'm sick if anyone asks . . . the flu. Yeah, the twenty-four-hour flu. Okay, I gotta go and practice being sick for my mom. How does this sound?

[*She makes a vomiting noise.*]

Pretty good, huh? And Abby, pray for me, please . . . What for? Are you kidding? That this volcano on my face is gone by tomorrow. Better yet, say a prayer with me now . . . Please?

[*She closes her eyes.*]

Our Father who art in heaven, hallowed be thy name. Thy kingdoms come, thy will be done, on earth as it is . . . at Central High. Give us this day our same seat at lunch, and taketh away this zit!

[*She opens one eye to look and see if it worked, but the frown on her face indicates the zit is still there.*]

VORTEXIA
Constance Congdon

Comic
VORTEXIA, 12 to 15

VORTEXIA, *an overweight girl, is auditioning to do a commercial for Burpee Ware to earn some money. But she just can't be "nice."*

VORTEXIA   Does anybody want some polyvinyl Burpee Ware? So this goes on this and you burp it. And inside is your two pieces of lettuce and your milligram of boiled chicken. Yum. I'm full. And in this one you can put your ten white grapes. Dessert! Oh no, not another one—*please*. I couldn't possibly eat *one more grape*! And then, if you ever go out to dinner, and have something left over from your daily allowance of three meats, four breads, and two fruits, or is it four fruits, two meats, and no breads? Because bread isn't the staff of life, you know—it's actually evil. It's made by Satan in his subterranean bakery. *Anyway*, if you have something left over when you're eating out and have put your fork down between each bite. Or, perhaps, you've been a really good girl and haven't picked up your fork in two or three years—if you have even a bite left over, you can put it in this purse-size polyvinyl Burpee Ware container and take it home to eat later, if you can take the anxiety and guilt of ever eating *again*. And then you can wash it out to use over and over—unless, of course, you've shoved it down the garbage disposal just to listen to it shred, like your pride has been shredded every time you eat or watch someone else eat while they lecture you on how to watch your weight and then give that big sigh after they've told you you have such a pretty face. And you can use your polyvinyl Burpee Ware containers for those homemade TV dinners of a piece of fish and green (by the time you've nuked them, gray) beans you can nibble at while you watch hours of soft-porn food ads and ads for diet pills and products presented by thin, thin women who are telling you what you should do about your problem, when they could be drug addicts . . . but, hey, they still look "good."

WAR IN PARAMUS
Barbara Dana

Seriocomic
THELMA, 15

THELMA *is a rebel. She is speaking to her school friends, Harry and Philip. THELMA's older sister is getting married. THELMA, Harry and Philip are hanging out in THELMAs living room.*

THELMA   She's marrying this guy? She doesn't even know if she likes him. And this thing . . . God. I didn't tell you about this. This thing about the silver bowls! She's all excited because her friend, Bev, got these wedding presents, a whole bunch of shit, including seven silver bowls! She registered at Orbachs, you may be interested to know. Why Orbachs didn't come clean and say Bev didn't need so many silver bowls I couldn't tell you. Anyway, Jennifer thinks these bowls are the best thing in the history of recorded time. It doesn't matter that Bev didn't know who the hell she was marrying, or why. She got seven silver bowls! So now she's a slave. She has to thank the seven people who sent the silver bowls she doesn't want and doesn't need. That's only polite. She has to buy the stationary, which has to be engraved with her new name because her old name isn't any good anymore because now she belongs to somebody else, she has to write the seven thank-you notes, she has to mail the seven thank-you notes, and then . . . care of the bowls! She has to polish these stupid bowls she doesn't want and doesn't need. That means getting the money to buy the polish, and replacing the T-shirt she tore up to make the rag she used to do the polishing. [*With growing intensity.*] See, it's not just the bowls. This kind of thing passes for life and it gives me the creeps. I get hamsters in

140

my veins. Bev's life! I'd rather kill myself! But that's what she wants. She doesn't have a clue. She's shriveled and died inside her idea of herself.

WAR IN PARAMUS
Barbara Dana

Dramatic
THELMA, 15

THELMA is speaking to her parents and her older sister. THELMA 's older sister is about to be married at the Ethical Culture Society. There have been intense struggles within the family, as all attention has been focused on THELMA 's sister. After a fight with her father the night before, THELMA left the house. She was out all night, returning the following morning after a failed attempt to rob Jiffy Donut with her friends. She has just been wrenched from her bed, where she had been curled up in a fetal position—cold, exhausted, unable to sleep—by her screaming and hysterical mother. Her parents are questioning her about what happened. They are in the living room.

THELMA   I was in the alley and my friends were there and Philip was throwing up and there was vomit and the dumpster and this starving cat was pacing around and I wanted to die! . . . My friends left . . . I didn't know what to do. I wished I had Harry's knife so I could slit my wrists! . . . It was hours . . . I was there and . . . I don't know, it was freezing and it smelled like shit . . . the dumpster and Philip's vomit. Then I remembered the matches. I took them from the counter at Jiffy Donut . . . and I was walking, walking . . . streets, stores, houses, nothing. Empty, endless, nowhere. And there was Ethical Culture. I looked at the building. I noticed how it's wood, like a house. That's good, I thought. Wood burns. I climbed the tree. I wanted to get on the roof. That's where I started the fire. [*Suddenly worried.*] Did the police call? I know they're going to call. They're going to call, or come to the door. I don't know why they're not here yet . . . Mr. Lombardi saw me. My gym teacher. He was putting out the trash. He looked at me and I ran. I had to get away from the fire and the roof and the porch! There's a porch, the top of the porch, and the screen frame, and I had the lighter fluid. I stole it from the 7-Eleven. I tore my shirt on the nail. It was a rag. I put it down on the edge of the porch frame. I picked up the lighter fluid. I poured it on the rag. I took the matches out of my pocket. I struck a match . . . and held it by the rag. It caught. And the flames! Right away, and I jumped back! It spread so fast! I had to get down the tree and I fell and I got up and I ran to the bushes! I was hiding and it wouldn't stop! It was so beautiful! So . . . REAL! . . . But the people came and I ran! Mr. Lombardi and the trash and I was running, but I couldn't! My knees, and I collapsed. I was on the sidewalk. I just lay there. [*Pause.*] Later, I went back to see. The smoke and the firemen and the lights and the tape . . . the people, the police. A lot of it burned. A third of it . . . I don't know . . . a wing. The whole thing is wrecked. I hid in the shed. Then I came home. [*Pause.*] So that's me, Mom. What do you think?

PLAY SOURCES AND ACKNOWLEDGEMENTS

Other Monologue and Scene Books

Best Contemporary Monologues for Kids Ages 7-15
edited by Lawrence Harbison
9781495011771 ....$16.99

Best Contemporary Monologues for Men 18-35
edited by Lawrence Harbison
9781480369610 ....$16.99

Best Contemporary Monologues for Women 18-35
edited by Lawrence Harbison
9781480369627 ....$16.99

Best Monologues from The Best American Short Plays, Volume Three
edited by William W. Demastes
9781480397408 ....$19.99

Best Monologues from The Best American Short Plays, Volume Two
edited by William W. Demastes
9781480385481 ....$19.99

Best Monologues from The Best American Short Plays, Volume One
edited by William W. Demastes
9781480331556 ....$19.99

Childsplay
A Collection of Scenes and Monologues for Children
edited by Kerry Muir
9780879101886 ....$16.99

Duo!
The Best Scenes for Two for the 21st Century
edited by Joyce E. Henry, Rebecca Dunn Jaroff, and Bob Shuman
9781557837028 ....$19.99

Duo!
Best Scenes for the 90's
edited by John Horvath, Lavonne Mueller, and Jack Temchin
9781557830302 ....$18.99

In Performance
Contemporary Monologues for Men and Women Late Teens to Twenties
by JV Mercanti
9781480331570 ....$18.99

In Performance
Contemporary Monologues for Men and Women Late Twenties to Thirties
by JV Mercanti
9781480367470 ....$16.99

The Monologue Audition
A Practical Guide for Actors
by Karen Kohlhaas
9780879102913 ....$22.99

One on One
The Best Men's Monologues for the 21st Century
edited by Joyce E. Henry, Rebecca Dunn Jaroff, and Bob Shuman
9781557837011 ....$18.99

One on One
The Best Women's Monologues for the 21st Century
edited by Joyce E. Henry, Rebecca Dunn Jaroff, and Bob Shuman
9781557837004 ....$18.99

One on One: Playing with a Purpose
Monologues for Kids Ages 7–15
edited by Stephen Fife and Bob Shuman with contributing editors Eloise Rollins-Fife and Marit Shuman
9781557838414 ....$16.

One on One: The Best Monologues for Mature Actors
edited by Stephen Fife
9781480360198 ....$19.

Scenes and Monologues of Spiritual Experience from the Best Contemporary Plays
edited by Roger Ellis
9731480331563 ....$19.

Scenes and Monologues from Steinberg/ATCA New Play Award Finalists, 2008–2012
edited by Bruce Burgun
9781476868783 ....$19.

Soliloquy!
The Shakespeare Monologue
edited by Michael Earley and Philippa Keil
9780936839783 Men's Edition ...$11.
9780936839790 Women's Edition ...$14.

Teen Boys' Comedic Monologues That Are Actually Funny
edited by Alisha Gaddis
9781480396791 ....$14.

Women's Comedic Monologues That Are Actually Funny
edited by Alisha Gaddis
9781480360426................$14.

Prices, contents, and availability subject to change without notice.